Praise for
The World Is About to Turn

"Dr. King once warned that 'we will either live together as brothers and sisters, or perish together as fools; the choice is ours, chaos or community.' In this new work, which authors Rick Rouse and Paul Ingram describe as a 'guidebook,' they reveal a glimpse into the chaos that has been part of our nation's life, while offering an intentional way to make a difference and create a true community that is God's dream for us."

—The Most Rev. Michael B. Curry,
Presiding Bishop of the Episcopal Church

"In this time of increased anti-Semitism and hate of all kinds, it is important for faith leaders to consider how our teachings contribute to the perpetuation of supremacy. Rick Rouse and Paul O. Ingram offer a rich tool in this work. *The World Is About to Turn* does not end at exploring history; it offers an authentic and relevant theology of inclusivity to support faith leaders in strengthening our communities and country with love and understanding."

—Rabbi Rachel Kort,
Temple Beth Or, Everett, WA

"There's a lot of fear and brokenness abroad in our land and in our hearts. It's a time when many wonder if the Christian faith has anything to say to our condition. Rick Rouse and Paul Ingram speak from a generous, benevolent, specifically Christian faith and give contemporary American Christians a word to say in the present moment. Here's a rare gift—a strong, hopeful, Christian witness."

—Will Willimon, United Methodist Bishop (retired),
Professor of the Practice of Christian Ministry, and author of
Who Lynched Willie Earle? Confronting Racism Through Preaching.

"As a Muslim, I am deeply inspired and moved by the authors' heartfelt compassion, profound moral courage, and practical wisdom to take right action and do my part in creating beloved community."

—Imam Jamal Rahman,
Director of Interfaith Community Sanctuary,
author of *Spiritual Gems of Islam*

"Rick Rouse and Paul Ingram have authored a book that is inspiring and beautifully written. *The World Is About to Turn* offers both history and hope, both truth and a path to transformation. It challenges us to rise to our best selves, resisting bigotry and phobias with love, unity, and compassion. The authors bridge our shared history to our current reality to our better destiny, pushing us toward authentic interfaith dialogue. This book offers humanity a new way of being with one another that is inclusive and honors the dignity and integrity of all. By answering two key questions—How did we get here? And where do we go from here?—this book leads us into a paradigm shift, a necessary undoing, and a universal recommitment to a faith that mends."

—**LaNesha DeBardelaben,**
Executive Director of Northwest African American Museum, Seattle

"I am pleased to heartily recommend this book from Rick Rouse and Paul Ingram. The many key problems they have identified for churches in the United States are experienced on a global scale. The spirits of white supremacy and extremism moving throughout the world, for instance, need prophetic challenge and correction. Rouse and Ingram have charted an important path."

—**Bishop Dr Munib A. Younan,**
Former President of the Lutheran World Federation, Jerusalem

"We live in an increasingly 'either/or' culture that demands absolute allegiance to one's position or cause and complete rejection of the other side. In *The World Is About to Turn*, Rick Rouse and Paul Ingram invite us to engage the reality of religious pluralism in America with humility and integrity. Humility lets us acknowledge that no human mind can comprehend the mind of God. Integrity calls us to bring our full selves, including our faith tradition, to the conversation. Rouse and Ingram give us a framework for genuine dialogue and fruitful cooperation."

—**The Rev. Elizabeth Eaton,**
Presiding Bishop, Evangelical Lutheran Church in America

"The divisive condition of our society yearns for this book with its message of love, equality, and oneness. We Buddhists also wholeheartedly support this message as represented in our metaphor of the Indra's Net of Jewels, wherein all the countless jewels on the net are interdependently connected and illuminating each other!"

—**Dr. Kenneth Kenshin Tanaka,**
Jodo Shinshu Buddhist (priest and scholar)

"Rick Rouse and Paul Ingram have created a remarkable tool of hope and insight. They offer a clear path to solid ground beyond our current quagmire of polarization. I appreciate the sound theological foundations upon which their thought is built. As a Bishop, I particularly welcome the pairing of a nuanced history with deliberate stepping stones of hope and repentance in which any congregation or small group can engage."

—The Rt. Rev. Megan Traquair, Bishop,
the Episcopal Diocese of Northern California

"Many open-minded Christians will learn much about their history of which they will genuinely try to repent. Rouse and Ingram cover, in a readable and comprehensive way, the information—most relevant for their intended audience— much of it still too little known."

—Dr. John B. Cobb, Jr.,
American theologian, philosopher, and environmentalist

The World Is About to Turn is a guide for all of us who are passionate about interfaith reconciliation, true community, and a way forward from divisiveness. Through story and practical suggestions, Rick Rouse and Paul Ingram move from the brokenness that exists in this country to claiming the hope that is before us in this informative and user-friendly book."

—The Rev. Shelley Bryan Wee, Bishop,
Northwest Washington Synod, Evangelical Lutheran Church in America

"This clearly written and engaging book seeks to address the distressing religious and ethnic hostility evident in today's society by offering religiously based recommendations for creating a just and compassionate community. In the face of attacks on churches, synagogues, mosques, and other places of worship, this book is an eloquent plea for constructive inter-religious dialogue, for building bridges of understanding and cooperation that serve the common good."

—Dr. Darrell Jodock, Professor Emeritus,
Gustavus Adolphus College

"In *The World Is About to Turn,* Rick Rouse and Paul Ingram ask the question 'How did we come to understand religion as a weapon that could be used against those who are different?' and then offer a road map to reclaiming a way of living faith that is just, peaceful and loving. Although the authors primarily focus on the United States, readers from other parts of the world can easily see parallels into their own lived realities. Most helpful of all are the questions at the end of each chapter for either self-reflection or small group study."

—The Rev. Susan Johnson, National Bishop,
the Evangelical Lutheran Church in Canada

"Rick Rouse and Paul Ingram have produced a prophetic and decisive word that is a clarion call to Christians in the Western world to a way of righteousness, faithfulness, and justice. Their analysis of all that besets the political and ecclesiastical domains is inspirationally insightful. The solutions they offer are a blueprint for the Christian movement. This is a comprehensive manifesto for a health-giving future for all, and especially the church. This is a must read for every preacher and Christian leader."

—Rev Dr. Ian T. Price,
International Publisher, MediaCom Education, Australia

"This is a hope-filled text for today . . . [and] a rich tapestry that weaves multiple religious traditions and wide-ranging resources into a coherent and compelling call to 'a life lived in response to the gracious acts of a loving God.' The clear prose, questions at the end of each chapter, and the constructive proposal for *10 Ways Forward* toward authentic dialogue across seemingly insurmountable differences offers a hope-filled future. A future where we engage in courage, freedom, and life rather than succumbing to fear, slavery, and death. This clarion call to honest conversation, humble action, and courageous engagement opens the way for the 'commonwealth of God' to flourish."

—Rev. Dr. Robin Steinke,
President of Luther Seminary, St. Paul, MN

"We could wish that the uncommon wisdom found in *The World Is About to Turn* were already the common sense shared by millions in our nation and world. But that-s the point of this powerful, insightful, and big-hearted book: if more of us are willing to reorient our minds and hearts, the world can indeed turn—toward justice, kindness, and deep spiritual humility. Chapter 7 alone is worth twice the price of this book. Enthusiastically recommended!"

—Dr. Brian D. McLaren,
author, speaker, activist

"Religion is a powerful force that influences the attitudes and behavior of human beings. Regrettably, it has been used all too often in our human history as a weapon of exclusion, of division, and even of hatred and warfare. This book charts a way whereby adherents of different religions may find common core values in their respective traditions and thus may be able to see through their differences, learn to respect one another in those differences, and find a way of mutual acceptance and cooperation. This book offers readers a way toward healing the wounded state of this nation and of our world, whereby we can all work together toward a peaceful and sustainable Earth community."

—Dr. Ruben L.F. Habito,
Perkins School of Theology, Southern Methodist University

"In an environment of increasing division and hostility often fueled by wayward expressions of religious fervor, Rick Rouse and Paul Ingram have issued a clarion call for people of faith to become bridge builders working together with others to improve our common life. *The World Is About to Turn* reckons with the social ills that plague us in a spirit of humility and offers specific practices and a path toward becoming a more compassionate and inclusive society characterized by mutual respect."

—Rev. Dr. Raymond Pickett,
Rector, Pacific Lutheran Theological Seminary, Berkeley

"With vivid detail and real-life examples, Rick Rouse and Paul Ingram investigate how our neighborhoods, churches, and nation have fragmented into competing factions and then provide specific community-building practices that generate healing and hope for the future. Drawing on teachings and images from many religious traditions, the reader is challenged to join with God in turning the world toward a more just and joyful path."

—The Rev. Richard Jaech, Bishop,
Southwestern Washington Synod, Evangelical Lutheran Church in America

"In our era of acrimonious division, Ingram and Rouse issue both a stinging critique of religion's role in our social problems and practical suggestions for how interreligious resources and initiatives can be part of the solution. An excellent resource for congregations and people of faith that will generate important discussions and action."

—Dr. Jamie Schillinger,
Professor of Islam/Ethics, Department Chair,
St. Olaf College, Northfield, MN

"America and the world at large are at a turning point. Core values like international law and human rights are eroding. Nationalism, racism, and religious exclusivism are on the rise. In such a context, it is easy to lose hope, heart, and direction. Rick Rouse and Paul Ingram provide a moral compass centered around justice, love of neighbor, and genuine dialogue; a much-needed guidebook for mending a nation's broken faith."

—Rev. Dr. Mitri Raheb,
Founder and President of Dar al-Kalima University
in Bethlehem. Palestine

"Rick Rouse and Paul Ingram have written an inspiring and very timely book that provides bridge-building strategies that enable those of faith or no faith to confront injustice in our society and create a hope-filled future. This valuable resource provides a basis for interfaith dialogue on some of the most important issues of our time, and I highly recommend that it be shared and discussed widely among all who care about the direction of our country and its faith-based institutions."

—Dr. Rod Schofield,
ELCA Representative to the Lutheran educational institutions in Jordan
and Palestine and Mediator for peace and understanding among
Jews, Christians, and Muslims

"In this important work, Rouse and Ingram have 'read the writing on the wall' of today's current events in order to articulate a clear and compelling call for renewal both in and through the church. Surveying the church's history, theology, and practices, they offer a realistic, and at times sobering, assessment of the church's complicity in too often adopting cultural prejudices. At the same time, they offer both rationale and resources for the church to be the community of faith, healing, and hope that God desires and the world desperately needs. Reading this work will push you to examine your presuppositions about what the church is, challenge you to stretch your vision of what the church can be, equip you to assist in bringing about necessary change, and encourage your faith in the God who continues 'to make all things new.'"

—Rev. Dr. David Lose,
Senior Pastor, Mount Olivet Lutheran Church, Minneapolis

The
W RLD
Is About to
TURN

The
WORLD
Is About to TURN

Mending a Nation's
Broken Faith

RICK ROUSE
PAUL O. INGRAM

Foreword by Peter Marty

CHALICE
P R E S S

SAINT LOUIS, MISSOURI
AN IMPRINT OF CHRISTIAN BOARD OF PUBLICATION

Bible quotations, unless otherwise noted, are from the
New Revised Standard Version Bible, copyright © 1989,
by Division of Christian Education of the National Council
of the Churches of Christ in the United States of America.
Used by permission. All rights reserved.
ChalicePress.com

ISBNs: 978-0-8272-3721-6 (print);
978-0-8272-3722-3 (ebook);
978-0-8272-3723-0 (ePDF)

*We dedicate this to our grandchildren
as well as to the other visionaries and dreamers
who will help make this world a better place,
for all people and for all of God's creation.*

Contents

Foreword by
Peter W. Marty

No shortage of opinions exists among people with differing ideas about the proper date of America's founding. When, exactly, were the seeds of the American experiment planted, seeds that would eventually form the distinctive shape we see in modern American life? Was it in 1776, the year that thirteen separate states declared their independence from Great Britain? Some people argue quite persuasively for 1789, when the US Constitution became the supreme law of the land. Then there is 1863, the year President Abraham Lincoln issued the Emancipation Proclamation, altering the legal status of 3.5 million enslaved African Americans; or 1865, when the outcome of the Civil War changed *these* United States to *the* United States of America. Some enthusiasts for America's immigrant origins prefer the significance of 1886, the year the Statue of Liberty was dedicated in New York Harbor; or 1903, when Emma Lazarus' famous sonnet was affixed to the statue's base. More recently, 1619 has gained favor as a date for our founding significance—the year enslaved people first began arriving by ship from West Africa.

For contemplating America's earliest underpinnings, my own preferred date of reference is 1630. In April of that year, while on board the ship *Arbella* en route to the Massachusetts Bay Colony, Puritan leader John Winthrop delivered the sermon, "A Model of Christian Charity." In it, Winthrop laid the groundwork for some of what later came to be known both positively and negatively as American exceptionalism. "We must bear one another's burdens. We must not look only on our own things, but also on the things of our brethren," he said. "We are entered into covenant with [God] for this work." Any breach of the covenant, which might occur through selfish or carnal pursuits in the present age, might well incite the wrath of God. Winthrop memorably referred to such wrath as a shipwreck.

> Now the only way to avoid this shipwreck, and to provide for our posterity, is to follow the counsel of Micah, to do justly, to love mercy, to walk humbly with God. For this end, we must be knit together . . . we must be willing to abridge ourselves of our superfluities, for the supply of other's necessities . . . we must delight in each other; make other's conditions our own; rejoice together, mourn together, labor and suffer together.

This common bond of mutuality would be tested many times over the centuries. Citizens of America have experienced both remarkable success and failure in making other peoples' condition their own. The report card for our nation is mixed when it comes to consistently and wholesomely rejoicing together, mourning together, and laboring and suffering together. Every chapter of American history has engaged its own form of the debate on whether "we the people" refers more to a profound sense of community or merely to a collection of individuals.

For those enamored with personal rights, a rugged individualism has defined American identity. Daniel Boone and Davy Crockett are emblematic heroes of this impulse. Marching to the beat of one's own drum, charting one's own course, and following one's own dreams in a spirited way has enabled many to embrace a life dominated by self-interest. In place of cherishing transcendent biblical ideals like those expressed by Winthrop, hyper-individualists typically are more interested in making sure they get a sufficient piece of the American pie they consider their own.

For those Americans who understand the good life to be something greater than a disparate group of lone rangers claiming their individual rights and autonomy, the common good remains a prized concept. In their best moments, these individuals believe that the well-being of the whole is as important, or more so, than their own well-being. Some of those who celebrate what Winthrop called "our bonds of [human] affection," understand that what they believe and think is not just their own business; it's also business that affects others. In other words, what's in their own hearts ends up impacting and shaping the ways they act in society. They consider both their citizenship and their faith to be something other than a self-project.

Any serious vision for mending a nation like ours, where the fabric of community gets frayed by competing religious and political forces, or sometimes shredded when those forces get weaponized, must include a deep sense of the way faith can inspire goodness. Not only do the best forms of faith teach us how to practice compassion and mercy; they also help us learn how to integrate acts of considerate justice for the sake of people who yearn for such.

Rick Rouse and Paul Ingram seem to grasp that *diversity* in and of itself is not a virtue. It's simply a demographic or geographic reality. When people with different backgrounds, languages, and identities live in relatively close quarters, there is diversity. The achievement of interfaith cooperation, however, does something with this diversity. It cultivates respect for people with different identities, encourages relationships between those who come from different tribes, and builds commitment among all toward a common good.

Dr. Martin Luther King Jr., in his *Letter from Birmingham Jail*, wrote about the ways in which we are all tied together despite our differences. We are all "caught in an inescapable network of mutuality," said King, "tied in a single garment of destiny. Whatever affects one directly, affects all indirectly. I can never be what I ought to be until you are what you ought to be, and you can never be what you ought to be until I am what I ought to be. This is the inter-related structure of reality."

From Winthrop's concept of covenant and mutual regard to King's inescapable network of mutuality, the American story is filled with promptings for its people to consider the needs and interests of others. For those who get excited by the prospect of building a life of meaning and possibility for the sake of other people enjoying similar goodness, this book serves as a fine resource. Only by threading our lives together with the divine gifts of justice, mercy, and humility will the torn or frayed fabric of our republic ever be mended.

—**Peter W. Marty, publisher,** *The Christian Century*

Preface

Honoring difference has never been easy, but it is a particularly complex issue for our time. The resurgence of racial, ethnic, and national loyalties in an increasingly interdependent world; tensions caused by social class, racial, ethnic, and gender differences residing in greater proximity; the consequences of growing diversity in our churches; relationships among the religions of the world; the impact of postmodernism on the normative visions we have used to manage difference; and the struggle to understand the meaning of reconciliation in conflicted contexts have all converged to mandate new approaches to diversity.

Dealing constructively with difference is also a new challenge for the mission of the church at the end of Christendom. Even as we continue to tell the Christian story in new ways, we must learn how to live without domination as partners and neighbors in a world in which Christianity and western enlightenment categories no longer predominate and in which there are many different ethnic traditions and religious options contending for allegiance on a shrinking planet. The agenda is comprehensive. It requires the best thinking from the social sciences and from theology in order to set a steady course through murky and sometimes turbulent water.[1]

—**Rev. Dr. Herbert E. Anderson, practical theologian**

Though I am small, my God, my all, you work great things in me,

And your mercy will last from the depths of the past to the end of the age to be.

Your very name puts the proud to shame, and to those who would for you yearn,

You will show your might, put the strong to flight, for the world is about to turn.

My heart shall sing of the day you bring.

Let the fires of your justice burn.

Wipe away all tears, for the dawn draws near,

And the world is about to turn . . .

From the halls of pow'r to the fortress tow'r, not a stone will be left on stone.

Let the king beware for your justice tears ev'ry tyrant from his throne.

The hungry poor shall weep no more, for the food they earn;

There are tables spread, ev'ry mouth be fed, for the world is about to turn . . .

"Canticle of the Turning" by Rory Cooney[1]

means of securing the support of this massive swath of religious-minded voters and their leaders. The recent attempt by Republicans to stack the US Supreme Court with conservative judges appears to be an effort to appease the "religious right" by turning back the clock on abortion rights and gay rights. Furthermore, religious belief and patriotism were seemingly intermingled. Taking the "right" political stand became the litmus test that proved you were a true American.

The president of Fuller Theological Seminary, Mark Labberton considers it a major crisis that the Evangelical movement has become so intertwined and identified with the "Religious Right." In addressing a national conference of evangelicals in the spring of 2018, Labberton stated:

> The central crisis facing us is that the gospel of Jesus Christ has been betrayed and shamed by an evangelicalism that has violated its own moral and spiritual integrity. . . . Today's egregious collusion between evangelicals and worldly power is problematic enough: more painful and revealing is that such collusion has been our historic habit. Today's collusion bears astonishing—and tragic—continuity with the past. Right alongside the rich history of gospel faithfulness that evangelicalism has affirmed, there lies a destructive complicity with dominant cultural and racial power. Despite deep gospel confidence and rhetoric, evangelicalism has become long-wedded to devastating social self-interest that defends the dominant culture over against that of the gospel's command to love the "other" as ourselves.[3]

Is Christianity in Crisis?

The largest growing category in studies of how Americans view their religious affiliation is "none"—no religious affiliation. According to research by the PEW Charitable Trusts, nearly a quarter of those surveyed now consider themselves not affiliated with any organized religion. And the number-one reason people give for that decision is that they don't think today's religious organizations share their values—values such as inclusion, economic justice, or even that science is real.[4]

Someone once said, "Two people you should never trust: a religious leader who tells you how to vote, and a politician who tells you how to pray." That could well be the mantra of many young people in our country today. Studies show that people in the younger generation—especially those in their twenties and thirties—are more progressive in their thinking than their parents and grandparents. They are more open-minded and justice oriented. At the same time, many would claim that they are spiritual but not religious.

This millennial generation tends to view institutional religion with suspicion and in some cases with distain.

Why are they shunning organized religion? Here are some of their assumptions: (1) religious people are hypocritical, judgmental, and insincere; (2) religions are partly true, but none is completely true; (3) religious organizations are too focused on rules, not on spirituality; (4) religious leaders only want money and power; and (5) religious people are anti-science.[5]

Linda Mercandante reports in her book, *Belief Beyond Borders*, that there are now more "none" in America than all the Protestants put together. She indicates that the largest percentage of the "none" or unaffiliated is among young adults, estimating that three-quarters of them identify with this category. She indicates that young people are now more religiously unaffiliated than earlier generations were at the same age. Her study further suggests that "a growing number of Americans have ceased to identify with, contribute to, or remain devoted to any particular religious tradition or faith community."[6]

Some of us believe Christianity is facing an identity crisis in this country and the Christian message itself is in peril. Is the purpose of the Christian faith primarily to gain power, enforce rules, or create wealth? Or is it to bring healing and hope to a broken world? People of all faiths would do well to ponder the following:

> God is not glorified by preventing refugees from receiving a life-giving avenue of escape. And God is not glorified by deporting immigrants. And God is not glorified by xenophobia. And God is not glorified by sexism. And God is not glorified by systemic racism. And God is not glorified by rejecting the maligned. And God is not glorified by fear, hate, shame, and pride.
>
> How can *salvation* be believed when we refuse to save refugees, or *hope* grasped when we deny it to immigrants, or *justice* pursued when we refuse it to the oppressed, or *faith* accepted when we don't have faith in those different from us, or *love* known when we deny it to our neighbors, strangers, and even our enemies?[7]

Where Do We Go from Here?

The changing religious and political landscape offers incredible challenges as well as opportunities. One needs only connect the dots to see how we arrived at our present situation of a polarized climate laced with bigotry, misogyny, and a lack of civility. Societal critics argue that America has lost its way, and we appear to have abandoned such core values as hospitality, fairness, and mutual respect. As a result, it appears Americans may be more divided today than during the years of the Civil War. How do we find common ground so that we can move forward together into a more just and hopeful future?

America was founded on a number of freedom principals that are embedded in the US Constitution. Among them are: (1) the freedom to practice one's religion without fear of persecution; (2) the freedom of speech and the right to express ones opinion without fear of reprisal; (3) the freedom of the press to ensure that those in position of power are held accountable; (4) the freedom of public assembly that allows for citizens to legally gather in protest or to campaign for a cause they think is right; and (5) the freedom to bear arms in order to protect oneself and one's country. These freedoms were not necessarily carved out of the Judeo-Christian tradition as some believe but rather were intended to protect the citizens of a new land against the tyranny and abuse of power they had experienced in Europe. Most of all, these freedoms were intended for the "common good" in America and to promote the welfare of all its citizens. In our individualistic culture of today, that spirit has been lost on those who revel in the partisan divide, claiming their cause is righteous while demonizing those who disagree.

There is even a growing rift among those of the Christian tradition. Theologian Marcus Borg offers the following observation: "We live in a time of a deeply divided Christianity. Unlike fifty or a hundred years ago, the divisions are not primarily denominational. Rather, the major division is between what I call 'an earlier Christian paradigm' and an 'emerging Christian paradigm,' between a belief-centered way of being Christian and a transformational-centered way of being Christian. To use conventional labels, the division is between conservative and progressive Christians. The former are commonly called evangelical Christians, both by themselves and others. The latter are found mostly in mainline denominations."[8]

Most recently a group of spiritual leaders from mainline American Protestant denominations issued a manifesto called "Reclaiming Jesus: A Confession of Faith in a Time of Crisis." Michael Curry, Presiding Bishop and Primate of the Episcopal Church, and Jim Wallis of Sojourners have joined with twenty-two other prominent religious figures in challenging current political and religious assumptions. Their main argument suggests that those of the Christian persuasion must begin by understanding the basic message of Jesus and then measure all actions and pronouncements by the gospel's admonition to "love thy neighbor." Examples of this are highlighted in the document:

If each human being is made in God's image and likeness then Christians have a duty to repudiate "the resurgence of white nationalism and racism in our nation on many fronts, including the highest levels of political leadership. A belief that "we are one body" requires opposition to "misogyny" and "the mistreatment, violent abuse, sexual harassment, and assault of women." Because "how we treat the hungry, the thirsty, the stranger, the sick, and the prisoner is how we treat Christ," Christians must oppose "attacks on immigrants and refugees" and "cutting services and programs for the poor" accompanied by "tax cuts for the rich" . . .

This is a testing time for the country as a whole, but a moment presents a particular challenge to the Christian churches. . . . The battle within Christianity (and not just in the United States) can be defined in many ways. It is at least in part between those who would use faith as a means of excluding others on the basis of nation, culture, and, too often, race, and those who see it as an appeal to conscience, a prod to social decency—and, yes, as an invitation to love.[9]

There are also encouraging signs, especially among members of the wider religious community. For decades, mainline denominations have participated in what is known as the ecumenical movement which has been marked by such institutions as the National Council of Churches and the World Council of Churches. The purpose has been to promote understanding, respect, and appreciation among the different branches of the Judeo-Christian tradition. And in recent years, inter-religious dialogue has included those of other faiths such as Islam, Hinduism, Buddhism, Daoist, and Confucian traditions. The search for common values is a key to bringing people together from all walks of life whatever their ethnic, socioeconomic, or religious background.

We are proposing a way forward for a culture that has become confused and conflicted. The journey ahead is not easy, but it is possible with a change of heart and attitude. Walter Brueggemann offers a vision of what we might aspire to: "If we ponder our destination, perhaps it is to be to the neighborhood of shalom, the neighborhood of shared resources, of inclusive politics, or random acts of hospitality and intentional acts of justice, of fearless neighborliness that is not propelled by greed or anxiety or excessive self-preoccupation . . . a great departure from the greedy, anxious anti-neighborliness of our economy, a great departure from our exclusionary politics that fears the other, a great departure from self-indulgent consumerism that devours creation."[10] The promise of our society lies in our ability to envision a new future that is just, fair, and true. We will explore that future together in the remaining pages of this book.

We close this chapter with a powerful commentary by Langston Hughes, an African American poet (1902–1967). "Let America Be America Again" was written in 1935. In it, he suggests the dream of America is yet to be fulfilled. Consider the context of this poem: America was in the midst of a Great Depression, and Europe was on the brink of World War II. Hughes captures the profound human struggle that continues today and suggests that perhaps America has yet to live into its promised future.

> O, let America be America again—
> The land that never has been yet—
> And yet must be—the land where every man is free.
> The land that's mine—the poor man's, Indian's, Negro's.
>
> ME—
> Who made America
> Whose sweat and blood, whose faith and pain,
> Whose hand at the foundry, whose plow in the rain,
> Must bring back our might dream again ..
>
> Sure, call me an ugly name you choose—
> The steel of freedom does not stain.
> From those who live like leeches on the people's lives,
> We must take back our land again,
> America!
>
> O, yes,
> I say it plain,
> America never was America to me,
> And yet I swear this oath—
> America will be[11]

Questions for Reflection

1. How has religion been used as a "weapon" to intimidate or manipulate people?

2. How do you think myths like the "doctrine of discovery" or "manifest destiny" have contributed to the notion that America is God's chosen nation?

3. What are some examples of the way politics and religion have become comingled? How can this be a dangerous thing?

4. Can you describe the reasons for the religious and political divide in this country?

5. Why is the manifesto "Reclaiming Jesus" a hopeful sign? Are there other hopeful signs?

2

When Justice Rolls Down

*Finding the Moral Courage
to Do What Is Right*

True peace is not merely the absence of tension,
but the presence of justice.

—Martin Luther King, Jr.

The Nightingale is a powerful story of individuals finding the moral courage to do the right thing during a time of war and oppression. Many chose to join the French resistance movement during World War II in order to oppose the injustices of the Nazi occupation. In one scene, one of the main characters, Vianne Mauriac, turns to her daughter, Sophie, and says, "Love has to be stronger than hate, or there is no future for us."[1] One could say the same about America today. With the alarming rise of hate crimes in the United States and the sense that we are living in an increasingly violent culture, one has to wonder what kind of a future we have as a nation.

We live in anxious times. Terrorists, politicians, and even religious leaders play on people's fears. In an attempt to push their agenda or manipulate the outcome they want, individuals and groups create scapegoats. They promote fear of the other, be they Muslims, Jews, African Americans, the LGBTQ community, or Latinos seeking asylum at our US–Mexico border. It's a tactic called "fear mongering." And although it has always been part of our historical past—the demonizing of various ethnic groups such as Native Americans, or African Americans, or those who came as immigrants such as the Irish, the Chinese, the Japanese, etc.—this strategy seems to have risen to new heights in recent years. Especially in a time when their "white privilege" is threatened and those who have been in the majority find themselves increasingly in the minority as the nation becomes more ethnically diverse.

Currently White Americans make up slightly more than half of the US population; however, the US Census Bureau predicts that by 2044 they will be in the minority. According to research done by the Pew Research Center, 46 percent of whites fear that this will weaken American culture. The report printed in *USA Today* goes on to state that "roughly half of Americans say a majority nonwhite population would lead to more racial and ethnic conflict."[2] The loss of white power and privilege has led to a rise in anti-immigration and nationalistic sentiment in the United States, Europe, and Australia where politicians and others fan the flames of anxiety and bigotry. Jack DeWaard, a sociology professor at the University of Minnesota suggests that while anti-immigrant views are not new in the United States, "What seems to be different is there's sort of a politics of fear and resentment. . . . The issue of migration has become so much more politicized, hijacked and divorced from facts and reason than it ever has in the past."[3] DeWaard goes on to explain that the fears of those in the majority becoming the minority are exacerbated when people don't interact meaningfully with those who are different from them.

Fear of the Other

Because I am an "other" to someone who is "other" to me, we are all "other" to one another. If that is true, then no one is a stranger, and yet we are all strangers to one another. Nonetheless, as practical theologian Herbert Anderson has suggested, we still use the word **Other** "to identify the one whom we believe is stranger or whom we perceive to be alien. . . . In this sense, the Other is someone who is different, who is *not like me*. The Other may be *not like me* in many ways, but the underlying assumption remains the same. If I am the norm for how the Other should act or what the Other should be, they, the ones outside, will always be strangers or the Others. The human impulse to determine who is IN and who is OUT, who is US and who is THEM has as its larger aim determining identity and belonging. We are included to say that we belong with people who are like us, and people who are not like us are outsiders because they are *not like me*." Anderson goes on to say that it is *a risk of being changed* by the Other "that evokes fear and despair in people and cultures who have presumed to have the normative view. Celebrating diversity and reinforcing particularity as an alternative to universalizing often surfaces an antiglobal point of view."[4]

Xenophobia is exclusionary fear of the Other. While most of us feel most comfortable hanging out with people who are like us, this kind of fear is more than mere discomfort of those who are different. It is about a deep fear of the Other when "we separate ourselves from others in order to better oppress, exploit, expulse, confine, hurt, or deny justice and access to others whom we have judged to be so Other as to be beyond the bounds of having any bond between us or any claim upon us."[5] This kind of deep-seated fear can lead to a demonizing and a dehumanizing of anyone or any group identified as the Other.

Fear of the other is compounded by several factors that include religion and economics. With the exception of the Roman Catholic Church, the largest Christian denominations in this country are primarily made up of people of Northern European descent. They have in many ways made God in their own image and are more comfortable with a "white" Jesus who looks and acts like them. Unfortunately, this view of religion has fed racial bigotry and led many to justify white supremacy. The late theologian James H. Cone challenged our history of burning crosses and lynching when he wrote: "While the lynching tree is seldom discussed or depicted, the cross is one of the most visible symbols of America's Christian origins. . . . Until we can see the cross and the lynching tree together, until we can identify Christ with a 're-crucified' black body hanging from a lynching tree, there can be no genuine understanding of Christian identity in America, and no deliverance from the brutal legacy of slavery and white supremacy."[6]

Those who have felt left behind economically—especially with the shuttering of steel mills, coal mines, and industrial plants in the heartland—are eager to find someone to blame as the American dream slips away from them. These folks feel especially vulnerable, often living on the edge from paycheck to paycheck. To compound their struggle, the opioid epidemic has claimed thousands of their loved ones. Many are also threatened by changes in societal norms that they see as a threat to their way of life. Rather than hope for a better tomorrow, they only fear for the future. That fear can lead to hate, which can turn to violence. How does one break this hopeless cycle and find a way forward?

A New Future

The Apostle John wrote these profound words of hope: "There is no fear in love, but perfect love casts out all fear" (1 John 4:18). He offered a vision for a new future based not on fear but on God's extravagant love for humanity and all of creation. In these next three chapters we seek to outline a new vision for life together based on this premise, using a passage from the Old Testament Prophet Micah to frame a way going forward.

With what shall I come before the Lord and bow myself before God on high?

Shall I come before him with burnt offerings, with calves a year old?

Will the Lord be pleased with thousands of rams, with ten thousands of rivers of oil?

Shall I give my firstborn for my transgression, the fruit of my body for the sin of my soul?

He has told you, O mortal, what is good; and what does the Lord require of you

But to do justice, and to love kindness, and to walk humbly with your God? (Micah 6:6–8)

God accuses the people of Israel of neglecting the covenant made with them at the time of Abraham and later confirmed with Moses. They have forgotten about God's deliverance from Egypt and God's promises going forward. Instead of trusting God, their leaders have trusted in equipment for battle, fortified cities, and even other gods. When the prophet Micah confronts them with God's disappointment and anger, they defend themselves before God by pointing to their religious practices. The prophet responds on behalf of God by arguing that these rituals are meaningless unless there is a genuine change of heart that in turn is put into acts of *justice, kindness, and humility*.

The more literal translation from the Hebrew suggests: "Do justice, live compassionately, and work for solidarity of community—founded on justice and compassion" (Paul Ingram's translation). The prophet is lifting up a way of living in community that is based on the values of justice, compassion, and humility. He is also a calling us to a life lived in response to the gracious acts of a loving God. This calls us to consider the true character of God or how one understands the nature of God. If one believes the teachings of the Jewish prophets and Jesus in the gospels—not to mention the teachings of other religious traditions—one would conclude the presence of God is found in all that is life-giving and love-affirming. Finally, it requires a radical transformation—a reorientation if you will—to a different way of living that treats all people and all of creation with respect and care.

Where Is the Justice?

It is easy to view the injustice in our nation and in our world. During the writing of this book, we have witnessed several horrific events. Fifty people were killed by a terrorist attack on two mosques in Christchurch, New Zealand. The victims included Muslim immigrants who had fled Somalia and

Syria in search of a safe haven they thought to be New Zealand. The perpetrator was a self-proclaimed White nationalist from Australia who claimed he wanted to make the world a safer place for people of Northern European descent. A few weeks later, an Islamist group from Sri Lanka walked into three Christian churches and three luxury hotels on the island and blew themselves up, killing more than 350 people. *The Economist* reported, "The aim of such sectarian terrorism is to promote the narrative of a clash of civilizations—an aim the jihadists share with white-nationalist terrorists. . . . Both groups want to sow discord and force people to choose sides."[7]

Where is the justice when people are unable to worship without fear whether it be in a mosque, a temple, or a church? Where is the justice when thousands of refugees must flee their countries of origin because of war, famine, or persecution only to be warehoused indefinitely in holding camps? Where is the justice when working-class women and men see the value of their wages shrink while the rich become wealthier? Where is the justice when we see our lands scarred and water polluted by greedy corporations? Where is the justice when 60 percent of the prison population in this country is made up of African Americans? Where is the justice if millions of US citizens in the richest country in the world do not have access to health care? Where is the justice when hundreds of migrant children are taken from their parents and kept in unsanitary conditions?

It is important to recall what *justice* is all about. The term can be defined broadly as: (a) just behavior or treatment—such as a concern for justice, peace, and genuine respect for people; (b) the quality of being fair and reasonable; and (c) the administration of the law or authority in maintaining this (justice). According to *Black's Law Dictionary*, justice has to do with protecting rights and punishing wrongs. But the dictionary suggests that it is possible to have unjust laws, even with fair and proper administration of the law of the land.[8] According to the Bible, God's justice or righteousness is often seen as God's acts of mercy. And justice for humans means the relief of the oppressed or needy. In his article "What is Biblical Justice?" theologian Paul Louis Metzger suggests that a theology of justice flows from the heart of God:

> Biblical justice involves making individuals, communities, and the cosmos whole, by holding both goodness and impartiality. It stands at the center of true religion. . . . Justice flows from God's heart and character. As true and good, God seeks to make the object of his holy love whole. This is what motivates God throughout the Old and New Testaments in his judgements on sin and injustice. These judgments are both individual and corporate. . . . In our post-Christian setting, many skeptics view religion as corrosive, divisive, and a source of injustice. But the kind of

religion the Bible advocates is rooted in justice that flows from the heart of God. It seeks to bring all things into the wholeness of God. As those justified by faith in the God of all justice, we are to experience the wholeness that he brings and extend it [to others] as citizens of his kingdom.[9]

Christianity has far too long focused on individual sins and private behavior while ignoring and even sometimes supporting structural and systemic evils such as war, corporate greed, misogyny, income inequality, and abuse of creation. Most people of faith are unconsciously complicit in unjust systems that benefit them at the expense of others, especially those on the margins of society. Theologian Richard Rohr believes that the deepest changes that need to happen for justice to take root in one's heart and mind comes through contemplation that allows one to see that everything is made in the image of God—thus understanding the universal dignity we share with all other beings. Christians, in particular, need to move beyond giving intellectual assent to religious doctrine to the actual practice of their faith through concrete actions that offer love and hope in a broken world.[10]

Faith Communities and Justice

What does it mean to live in a community that acts with justice? Whether it be a religious or secular group, the first sign of justice is a willingness to have the conversation about what is just or unjust. It is disconcerting to note that approximately 60 percent of Christian congregations in the United States report that they do not discuss controversial issues.[11] This may be because the leadership is unwilling to "rock the boat" or stir up possible conflict. Some may simply not know how to invite people with different points of view into respectful conversation. The problem is that sweeping difficult issues under the rug can lead to denial, unresolved conflict, pain, and greater injustice. What if faith communities became a safe place for honest conversation? What if congregations provided a climate of openness and mutual respect in which people could share their deepest fears and greatest hopes?

One of the issues that people of faith may struggle with is a reluctance to "let go" of the past or go outside of their comfort zone. Walter Brueggemann writes,

Moaning and grieving and weeping have to do with relinquishment, about which we are always reluctant. I think, speaking to that point that the church's struggle about welcoming gays and lesbians [for example] is not much about sexuality. It is about clinging to an old world we could manage wherein we felt safe. We always fight a rearguard action against relinquishment: if not gays, then Muslims, and if not Muslims, then immigrants, and after immigrants we will find new candidates around whom to draw a line against relinquishment. It is a common temptation among conservatives and among liberals, for nobody I know wants readily to give up what we treasure.[12]

He goes on to suggest that congregations become a venues for processing loss and acknowledging a world that is no longer. For it is in the processing of grief that hope and new life are born.

We hope that people of faith would be willing to engage in conversation about difficult issues, even when they face pushback. Recently one congregation in the Seattle area advertised on social media that they were holding a seminar on racism to which members of the community were invited. They began to receive threats of violence from an individual who opposed this event. Yet faith communities are called to take the risk and to take the lead in educating people regarding justice issues. *Neighbors in Faith*, an interfaith group in Seattle, has held more than sixty "faith over fear" seminars in the past two years—providing a forum where members of different faith traditions and of various political persuasions can come together for the purpose of finding ways to better understand one another and to work together for justice in the larger community.

Communities that act for justice are filled with individuals who seek to make a difference for good in the wider world. In a time of challenge or crisis, they respond with positive action rather than with a knee-jerk reaction of fear and anger. One example was offered by the students of Marjory Stoneman Douglas High School in Parkland, Florida. When a lone gunman killed teachers and fellow students in an act of senseless violence in February of 2018, many of the students took up the cause of stricter gun control laws while others led a campaign to register more young voters. In response to the murders in a New Zealand mosque, a friend from Auckland wrote these words: "As fearful as this type of horror makes me, it also makes me more determined to reach beyond ridiculous human-made walls of country, religions, race, gender, sexual preference, etc., to build a world with far more good than bad, with more love than hate."

Justice as Resistance

Sometimes justice calls on people of faith to resist the power of evil. They must choose to stand with the powerless over standing against the powerful. Dietrich Bonhoeffer, a Protestant pastor and theologian who was martyred by the Nazis during World War II, did just that. He could not stand idly by when in 1933 the Protestant Church in Germany greeted the brutal exclusion of entire social groups as simply the "restoration of order." Bonhoeffer was a prophetic voice speaking for the victims stating that "the church has an unconditional obligation to the victims of any ordering of society, even if they do not belong to the Christian community. . . . Moreover, the church has the possibility and the duty not just to bandage the victims under the wheel, but to put a spoke in the wheel itself."[13]According to German theologian, Renate Wind, this was Bonhoeffer's call for political resistance to a brutal regime, suggesting that the church throw itself between the spokes of the wheel in order to stop it.

Ten years later, Bonhoeffer wrote in a draft for a church confession of guilt—not made by the German churches until a half century later:

> The church was silent where it had to cry out . . . the church confesses that it had witnessed the lawless application of brutal force, the physical and spiritual suffering of countless innocent people, oppression, hatred and murder, and that it had not raised it voice on behalf of the victims and has not found a way to hasten to their aid. It is guilty of the death of the weakest and most defenseless brothers (and sisters) of Jesus Christ.[14]

Bonhoeffer chose the path of resistance to what he believed to be an unjust and cruel government. While the majority of German pastors took an oath of allegiance to Hitler, he became involved in a plot to overthrow Hitler and the Nazi regime. American theologian Mark Brocker writes,

> The heart of Bonhoeffer's resistance was his confidence in God's deep love for the world. That deep love was the firm ground on which he took his stand in resisting Hitler and the Nazis . . . Bonhoeffer makes abundantly clear that God's love is not directed toward some ideal world. God accepts the real world, the world as it actually exists, here and now, with all its sins and shortcomings.[15]

So what is the role of resistance for people of faith today? Does not justice require one to stand with the oppressed over standing against the oppressor? "The fitting response to injustice and tyranny must be discerned in the given circumstances of life. A person of faith accepts that in a suffering world, suffering is likely to be a consequence of one's efforts to resist. One must be willing to lay one's life and reputation on the line—even risk being wrong."[16] Brocker suggests that in Bonhoeffer's time, the major challenge was to wake people up to the destructive path Germany was going down, but today

> It is not enough simply to wake people up. To change an entrenched way of life, people need to be moved by something way down deep. For Bonhoeffer that something was God's deep love for the world. In this Christ moment, God's deep love for this world will truly be the driving motivation for followers of Jesus intent on engaging in acts of resistance.[17]

For the person of faith, acts of resistance are motivated by God's desire for justice born out of love and that good ultimately triumph over evil.

Advocates for Justice

The *Nordic Way* describes values common to people who hail from Scandinavian countries. These include a strong sense of justice and fairness, stewardship of nature, openness, equality, tolerance, and respect for every human being.[18] From this sense of justice, comes a desire to make the world a better place, a place where people can live together in peace and harmony. It is not surprising that diplomats from countries such as Norway have been engaged in peace-making efforts in Northern Ireland, South Africa, the Middle East, and elsewhere around the world. The Oslo Accords, for example, were a set of agreements between the Palestinian Liberation Organization (PLO) and the government of Israel signed in Washington, DC, in 1993 that aimed at fulfilling the right of Palestinian people to self-determination. Furthermore, each year the Nobel Peace Prize is awarded in Oslo to persons or organizations that is recognized for their efforts in promoting peace and justice. Likewise, the United States has been known in the past as an advocate for human rights, justice, and peace around the globe. What will it take for us to reclaim this role?

Justice has been a prevailing theme in the ongoing struggle for individual rights as well as religious and economic freedom in America. During the 1960s, prominent leaders of the Civil Rights Movement including Dr. Martin Luther King Jr. often quoted from the prophet Isaiah: "Let justice roll down like waters, and righteousness like an ever-flowing stream" (Amos 5:24). Those ancient words still resonate today as communities of faith are challenged to step out of their comfort zones and boldly take a stand for what is right and just. Even if this means standing with the weak rather than always considering first the right of the strong and powerful. William Whitla wrote the text for a hymn that reflects this call for justice in 1989 right after the events in Tiananmen Square and about the time the Mothers of the Disappeared in Argentina were making an appeal on the world stage, It is a powerful reminder of the need to stand for justice:

> *Let streams of living justice flow down upon the earth;.*
> *Give freedom's light to captives, let all the poor have worth.*
> *The hungry's hands are pleading, the workers claim their rights,*
> *The mourners long for laughter, the blinded seek for sight.*
> *Make liberty a beacon, strike down the iron pow'r,*
> *Abolish ancient vengeance; proclaim your people's hour.*[19]

Questions for Reflection

1. What are some of the things that can contribute to "fear of the other"?

2. Describe some examples of injustice in our nation and in our world today?

3. What does "Biblical justice" consist of? Where does it originate?

4. How can faith communities become instruments of justice?

5. In what ways can the act of resistance contribute to bringing about justice

3

Love One Another

Practicing Mercy and Compassion

> Preaching that we are to **love** our neighbor, **welcome**
> the stranger and **stand up** for the marginalized does
> not mean you are making **political** statements. It
> means you are making **Biblical** statements.
>
> **—a Southern Baptist pastor**

Three thousand of us gathered at a mosque in Redmond, Washington—Christians, Sikhs, Buddhists, Jews, and even nonbelievers joined our Muslim brothers and sisters in the aftermath of the deadly massacre in New Zealand that left fifty worshippers dead. Our response to hate was to strengthen one another in love.

A few weeks later, many of the same people met at St. James Catholic Cathedral in Seattle in response to the massive murder of Christians in Sri Lanka. Worshippers processing out of the cathedral with candles for a prayer vigil in the courtyard were met by their Muslim friends who handed out bouquets of flowers. It was their way of saying, "We are so sorry for what has happened to our Christian sisters and brothers." Believing that God takes what was intended for evil and can use it for good, we recognized that we were all beloved children of God.

The Hebrew scriptures remind us that God created a world with a rich diversity of people and ethnic groups. The Prophet Daniel shared a vision in which all nations, all peoples, all languages serve together.[1] An example of various ethnic and faith traditions working side by side was reported by Good Shepherd Lutheran Church in Alexandria, Virginia. They invited members of a local mosque to join them in a community service project where together they packaged twenty thousand meals for the hungry.

There are multiple incidents of people from diverse backgrounds and of different faith traditions coming together to face a community tragedy or challenge. Whether it is the aftermath of a tornado, flood, fire, or a mass shooting, people seem able to put their differences aside and rally to a common cause. Some individuals seem able to practice random acts of kindness on a daily basis even when there is no crisis at hand. They take to heart the prophet Micah's plea to love kindness and act with compassion toward others.[2]

Acting with Kindness and Compassion

What does it mean to be kind or compassionate to others? It is helpful to consider what the Merriam-Webster Dictionary has to say. A person who is "kind" is described as having a sympathetic or helpful nature, a forbearing nature, and one who is gentle. It also means to give pleasure or relief, to be affectionate and loving. A "compassionate" person is one who has a sympathetic consciousness of others' distress together with a desire to alleviate it; one who shows mercy.

A perfect example of someone with these characteristics is found in the Parable of the Good Samaritan as told by Jesus in the New Testament:

Just then a lawyer stood up to test Jesus. "Teacher," he said, "what must I do to inherit eternal life?" He said to him, "What is written in the law? What do you read there?" He answered, "You shall love the Lord your God with all your heart, and with all your soul, and with all your strength, and with all your mind; and your neighbor as yourself." And he said to him, "You have given the right answer; do this, and you will live."

But wanting to justify himself, he asked Jesus, "And who is my neighbor?" Jesus replied, "A man was going down from Jerusalem to Jericho, and fell into the hands of robbers, who stripped him, beat him, and went away, leaving him half dead. Now by chance a priest was going down that road; and when he saw him, he passed by on the other side. So likewise, a Levite, when he came to the place and saw him, passed by on the other side. But a Samaritan while traveling came near him; and when he saw him, he was moved with pity. He went to him and bandaged his wounds, having poured oil and wine on them. Then he put him on his own animal, brought him to an inn, and took care of him. The next day he took out two denarii, gave them to the innkeeper, and said, 'Take care of him; and when I come back, I will repay you whatever more you spend.' Which of these three, do you think, was a neighbor to the man who fell into the hands of the robbers?" He said, "The one who showed him mercy." Jesus said to him, "Go and do likewise." (Luke 10:25–37)

This passage from Luke's Gospel is rich in meaning, and it is as contemporary and applicable today as it was in first-century Palestine. The story answers the question put to Jesus: "Who is my neighbor?" It suggests that whoever we discover is in need, there we will find our neighbor. The twist that Jesus adds to the lesson is that it was a Samaritan—a clan of people often reviled and viewed as suspect by Jewish religious leaders of the day—who was the real hero of the story. It was not one of their own; it was not a Levite, a teacher of the law, nor was it a priest. They both avoided the man who had been robbed and left for dead. Perhaps because they were afraid of being defiled and made unclean by touching a corpse. It was left to a traveling Samaritan to bind up the victim's wounds and provide for his care, thus acting as the true neighbor.

The surprising development in the story is that it is the Other, the despised Samaritan, who is lifted up as the example of what it means to be a good neighbor. Bishop Will Willimon suggests that this is not so much a story of who we are to be a neighbor to, but rather about who is a neighbor to *us*.

> Who is the Other coming toward me, the scary Other whom I fear who just might save me if I were to risk embrace? We are dying in a ditch, proud and alone. Our unexpected neighbor is the one whose love is so extravagant that it saves. Here is a story, not about the difficulty we good ones face in deciding who deserves our neighborliness, but the difficulty we all have in seeing this despised stranger, this Other . . . as neighbor.[3]

Another reason this moral lesson is so radical is because the designation for "neighbor" in the Hebrew tradition applied in that day to those among the covenanted people of God, the Jews. The admonishment to care for the neighbor meant to be kind to and show mercy to those of the same culture and faith. It could also be extended to include proselytes, those who were in the process of becoming part of the Jewish faith. However, some Jewish leaders of the day felt that the term "neighbor" (*plesion* in the Greek) should include all who were created in God's image, to all of humankind regardless of race or creed. Greek Archbishop Dmitri writes, "The lawyer's question ['Who is my neighbor?'] does not necessarily reflect a personal uncertainty, as much as it does the controversy being debated at the time."[4]

Jesus makes it clear that the term "neighbor" be understood in the broadest sense of the word and not be restricted to one's own kind. The neighbor in this parable is not only the object of compassion but includes the person who has shown mercy to another—the Good Samaritan. Furthermore, when Jesus says to the young lawyer "go and do likewise" he suggests that the neighbor is everyone with whom we come in contact, especially someone in need.

The Protestant reformer, Martin Luther, taught that we best show our love for God by loving the neighbor in need. He suggested that anyone who needs our mercy and compassion—without judgment about whether the person deserves it and without regard for who they are—is our neighbor.[5] And if we love God with all our heart and mind, every human being is viewed as a neighbor and can become an opportunity for showing love to God. Luther's teaching echoes that of John the Evangelist:

> Beloved, let us love one another, because love is from God; everyone who loves is born of God and knows God. Whoever does not love does not know God, for God is love . . . We love because God first loved us. Those who say, "I love God" and hate their brothers or sisters, are liars; for those who do not love a brother or sister whom they have seen, cannot love God whom they have not seen. The commandment we have from him is this: those who love God must love their brothers and sisters also. (1 John 4:7– 8 and 19–21)

We interpret this passage from a universal perspective. If Jesus suggests that the neighbor is everyone we meet—regardless of religion, class, or ethnic background—then all of God's children must also be our "brothers and sisters." This is what is so radical or revolutionary about the teachings of Jesus and the Christian scripture. It tends to be all inclusive rather than exclusive. It propels us beyond our comfort zone to care for the downtrodden, the outcast, the misfits in life.

This truth is especially apparent when Jesus talks about the judgment of all the nations, when the righteous will be separated from the unrighteous:

> Then the king will say to those at his right hand, "Come, you that are blessed by the Father, inherit the kingdom prepared for you from the foundation of the world; for I was hungry and you gave me food, I was thirsty and you gave me something to drink, I was a stranger and you welcomed me, I was naked and you gave me clothing, I was sick and you took care of me, I was in prison and you visited me." Then the righteous will answer him, "Lord when was it . . . " And the king will

answer them, "Truly I tell you, just as you did it to one of the least of these, you did it to me." (Matthew 25:31–40)

Here Jesus seems to suggest that salvation comes even to those who do not know him but who have shown care and compassion especially for those on the margin who are among the suffering children of God.

Showing Love for the Stranger

One of the greatest tragedies of our time is the international refugee crisis. According to the United Nations High Commissioner for Refugees, 68.5 million people have been displaced from their homes because of war, famine, natural disaster, and religious or political persecution. Of these, at least one third are refugees and a good number are children without families. Many are living in crowded refugee camps, while others are still in flight trying to find a place of refuge. Some nations have opened their borders to new immigrants while others are closing theirs. For context, US refugee admissions peaked in the 1980s, welcoming some 200,000 annually. Yet today when the need is so great, the US administration has set the ceiling for refugee arrivals at 30,000 a year; while Canada, on the other hand, has agreed to welcome around 330,000.

The challenges of resettlement of refugees in another country are many. It has been compounded by those who have politicized the problem and are demonizing refugees and migrants. They promote fear of the Other by suggesting that these strangers are mostly made up of criminals, rapists, drug dealers, and terrorists. In 2017, a whole swath of countries in which Islam is the predominate religion were banned by the US Immigration Service, including such countries as Yemen where searing conflict and extreme poverty have forced 3 million people to flee. This ban was upheld by the US Supreme Court, and additional countries have since added to the list by the Trump administration.

The crisis at the southern border of the United States has only increased. In the spring of 2020 the White House actively closed all entry points from Mexico and refused to consider any appeals for asylum. And using the COVID-19 pandemic as the primary reason, all immigration from outside the United States was halted indefinitely. Meanwhile, children who had been separated from their parents are still being held in containment facilities, often in unsanitary conditions. The *Washington Post* reported in June of 2020: "Overcrowding and unsanitary conditions in CBP border stations grew dire, and the deaths of seven children in less than one year put addition pressure on lawmakers to provide the border agency with the emergency funds it was seeking."[6] The psychological and emotional toll being taken on these young people has to be incalculable.

What seems easily forgotten is that these strangers are also children of God. Peter Marty, publisher of *The Christian Century*, writes, "On this matter of the stranger, we should learn from the ancient Jews. Only once does the Hebrew Bible contain the command to love the neighbor (Leviticus 19:18). More than thirty-five times, though, these same scriptures command one to love the stranger. Why the emphasis on the stranger? 'Our neighbor is one we love because he is like ourselves,' says Rabbi Jonathan Sachs. 'The stranger is the one we are taught to love precisely because he is not like ourselves.' The drumbeat of distain for immigrants today—foreign-born individuals who appear strange to us—is deplorable."[7]

The Hebrew and Christian scriptures are filled with stories of migrants and refugees. The Exodus—a central story in the Old Testament—recounts the flight of the Israelite slaves from Egypt and their migration to Canaan. In the New Testament, Joseph and Mary flee Herod's persecution to seek refuge in Egypt with their infant child, Jesus. It was also a Middle East tradition in biblical times (and still is today) to show hospitality to strangers—to offer a meal and even lodging to those passing through. And just as important, they were to welcome newcomers—even foreigners—into the community as suggested in Leviticus 19:34: "The alien who resides with you shall be to you as a citizen among you; you shall love the alien as yourself, for you were aliens in the land of Egypt: I am the Lord your God."

The Wing Luke Museum in Seattle seeks to share the story of Asian Pacific immigrants, how many were labeled as aliens and made to feel like outsiders. There were challenges, conflicts, and hardships that included the internment of thousands of men, women, and children with Japanese ancestry during World War II. For many Asian Pacific Americans, the questions of identity, home, and connection continue to be especially meaningful. Their stories ask us to consider the limits of our own ways of thinking and what we can learn when we open ourselves to another's worldview.

People of all faith traditions and of different ethnic backgrounds are called to embrace the stranger and to welcome the Other as a child of God. As we have recounted, our nation has not always been kind to those who appeared different from those early settlers, the majority of whom were Northern European and followers of the Protestant expression of the Christian faith. Catholics and Jews, LGBTQ+, and people of color have all endured bigotry and persecution of some kind in a country that claims to be "the land of the free and the home of the brave." We need to move beyond our fear and distrust of the other, those who are different from us. It is past time to accept the richness of our diversity as a nation and learn how to practice genuine hospitality to all.

Practicing Hospitality

Sometimes we have an experience that enlightens and surprises. In the fall of 2013, group of pastors and educators from across the United States went across the border into Mexico with an organization called Border Link. It was billed as an immersion event, designed to help us better understand the immigration issue. We spent a day visiting with many people from different walks of life. We went to a factory to talk with both workers and managers and we discussed wages and working conditions. We had a conversation with community leaders including a social worker and the town's mayor both of whom shared with us ways they were trying to improve the quality of life in the community. Then in smaller groups of three or four, we were taken to makeshift dwellings near the town dump.

We were invited into the homes of families living in abject poverty. They had constructed shelters made of cardboard walls and tin roofs built over dirt floors. The "house" we entered consisted of two small rooms. One was a gathering space furnished simply with a table and chairs, and the small kitchen was made up of a propane stove, some cupboards, a basin for washing, and an ice chest. A friendly Hispanic woman in her early thirties welcomed us and urged us to be seated. Two young children—a girl and a boy between the ages of six and ten—appeared in the doorway of the next room, which appeared to serve as the family sleeping quarters. They were wearing clean clothes, their hair was carefully brushed, and they smelled of ivory soap. They greeted us politely in English and then helped their mother serve us lunch.

A large bottle of Coca-Cola appeared on our table along with four glasses. Paper plates with fresh, warm tortillas were handed to each one of us. Then the woman brought a pan from the stove that was filled with shredded chicken and spices which she ladled onto our tortillas. It was all very delicious. One of our group served as a translator, and we talked with the woman about her family's situation. She told us that her husband worked for minimum wage at the local factory, and the children attended a Catholic parochial school in town. They were people of faith who were active in their local parish. And although they had very little, they were grateful for what they had. The generosity and hospitality shown to us that day both amazed and humbled us.

There are many examples that could be shared of people from humble means who practice genuine hospitality. In many cases, it comes from a deep sense of gratitude to God for the simple blessings of life. Often this is experienced among those communities that are less affluent, be they in this country or other parts of the world. It is both interesting and true that the more people have, the more they desire, and the less content or grateful they seem to be. True hospitality also stems from the valuing of human relationships. Most people hunger for a genuine sense of community and a place to belong. Like the television sitcom *Cheers*, they long for a place where everybody knows their name and where they can be accepted and loved for who they are.

Some faith communities seek to practice radical hospitality and be welcoming to all. A sign in in the narthex of the Holy Spirit Lutheran Chruch (Kirkland, Washington) announced,

> We welcome DIVERSITY of race, culture, spirituality, gender, identity, ability, and orientation. WE SEEK to provide a safe and inclusive place for all. WE REJECT intolerance and any form of degradation, hurt, or abuse. WE COMMIT in words and actions to uphold the rights of all to feel safe, valued, and respected. Within this space, love, peace, and understanding unify us.[8]

This is certainly a worthwhile goal, something to aspire to. It may seem unrealistic to some and unattainable to others. Yet while this statement sets the bar high, and it reveals the kind of community that this group of faith-filled people desire to be. It gives them a sense of identity as a welcoming and safe place for all people. And it perhaps reminds them of the hard work that is required to model such grand hospitality.

Our faith communities as well as our neighborhoods would do well to emulate the YMCA as an example of how to practice hospitality for all. Recently many YMCA community centers have been remodeled with the expressed purpose of showing they welcome everyone. In the lobby of our local "Y," one will find the word "hello" painted on the wall in many different languages, including Arabic, Russian, and Chinese. On another wall, are words and phrases that describe the hopes and aspirations of the YMCA: "Building Global Community," "Respect Is Our Golden Rule," "Act as One," "Strength in Community," "United in Cause," "Y for All," and "Join Us and Make a Difference." Outside by the entrance a rainbow flag is proudly displayed as yet another sign that all people are welcome and included.

Many faith communities struggle to be such a welcoming place. They are often focused inward on themselves. They are not always very hospitable toward strangers. When a newcomer attempts to sit in the place where a regular member usually sits during worship, they may be asked to find a seat elsewhere. Long-time members often form cliques and speak only among themselves, ignoring someone who is new. A person who is not well-dressed or well-groomed may even be shunned. People who look or speak different may be viewed with suspicion. When this is the case, it doesn't matter how welcoming the verbiage on the outdoor sign or website—or even what may be posted in the lobby or what appears in the bulletin. True hospitality requires effort and an attitude of wanting to reach out to others. And yes, hospitality can be taught and can be learned. Sometimes it is simply learning how to listen to each other that can help transform a culture—from an inward focus to an outward one, one that is more welcoming and accepting of others. We will explore this in more detail in Chapter 7, "Building Bridges of Hope."

The Evangelical Lutheran Church in America became the first Protestant denomination in the United States to declare itself a "sanctuary" denomination. It did so at its 2019 Churchwide Assembly in response to US government policies and practices that include both the random deportation of illegals and mistreatment of those seeking asylum at our borders. In a letter to the congregations of the Northwest Washington Synod, Bishop Shelly Bryan Wee explained, "Becoming a sanctuary denomination means that the ELCA is publicly declaring that walking alongside immigrants and refugees is a matter of faith. Being a sanctuary denomination is about loving our neighbors. While we may have different ideas about how to fix this broken system and may have different ways of loving our neighbors, our call to love our neighbor is central to our faith."[9]

The bishop went on to suggest that being a sanctuary denomination will look different in different contexts. For example, in some cases it may mean providing space for people to live, providing financial and legal support to those who are working through the immigration system, hosting English as a Second Language (ESL) classes, or marching as people of faith against the detention of children and families. We made it clear that no congregation is being asked, expected, or required to break any laws. The sanctuary document also recognizes the decades-long work of Lutheran Immigration and Refugee Services (LIRS) and how Lutheran congregations put their faith into action through both advocacy and resettlement of refugees.

The sad truth is that in our age the word "sanctuary" has been called into question. People cannot be certain that our houses of worship are safe places let alone places of hospitality and welcome. We have cited examples of many who have been defiled by hateful acts of violence in this country and around the world. In 2019, a gunman who claimed to be a Christian killed a woman and wounded three during services at a synagogue in Poway, California. He then later told a 911 dispatcher he had done it because "the Jewish people are destroying the white race."[10] He admitted, like others before him, that he had

peaceful protests demanding systemic racism and police brutality to be addressed to fan the flames of a race war that he hopes will carry him to reelection."[3]

White Supremacists seem emboldened by the fierce rhetoric of some politicians and religious leaders. The country has seen a dramatic increase in the number of extremist and hate groups (e.g., white nationalists) along with a resurgence of the Ku Klux Klan. There has also been a rise in anti-Semitism and Islamophobia with acts of violence directed toward our Jewish and Muslim neighbors in their places of worship and community centers. Hostile passions have been enflamed regarding the influx of Latino migrants crossing the southern border and seeking refuge in the United States.

Many people have expressed their concern about how US Immigration Services are treating refuge seekers at the border, and especially about the way thousands of children have been separated from their parents. America has a sordid past when it comes to taking children from their parents. Consider how African babies born into slavery in this country were ripped from their parents' arms and sold to the highest bidder. Recall how Native American children were taken out of their homes at an early age and placed in Indian Residential Schools where their native identities and culture were wrenched away from them; and they were taught to behave as children of European immigrants. Where did such cruelty and hostility toward others originate? And how can it be overcome so that we can cauterize this deep wound in American culture?

The Sin of Arrogance

The Arts and especially theatrical productions often mirror the conflict in society of various ethnic groups trying to build a better life for themselves in spite of the barriers a racist culture has placed before them. *Small Island* opened to critical acclaim on the London stage in 2019. It is a powerful story about relationships and race set against the backdrop of the complex history of Jamaica and the United Kingdom. In one key scene, a black immigrant, Eustache, confronts Rothney, a proud and arrogant Englishman, about his prejudice and tendency to put down people of color:

> You know what your trouble is man?...Your white skin. You think it gives you the right to Lord is over a black man, but you know what it make you? White. That is all, man. No better, no worse than me.[4]

Nearly every society appears to have a superiority complex. It seems every country, nation, and tribe wants to believe that it is better than others and will choose to act in its own self-interest. That is one of the reasons for the legacy and scars of war left on the planet. So when Northern European powers began their worldwide expansion known as colonialism, they sought to impose the religion and culture of what they believed was a superior society. Christianity was the religion of the empire and was used unapologetically as a weapon of subjugation by both conquerors and missionaries. It could be argued, of course, that any religious group that seeks to put down others commits the sin of arrogance. And there is usually a power differential at work whenever one group declares that "We have the truth" at the expense of others.

> The Merriam-Webster Dictionary updated its definition of racism in 2020 to read: "A belief that race is the primary determinant of human traits and capacities and that racial differences produce an inherent superiority of a particular race."

The issue of religious or cultural superiority is addressed in the Judeo-Christian scriptures. The Old Testament implies that the Jews as God's Chosen People were given license to expand their territory and conquer the inhabitants. In the New Testament, we witness the prejudice of the Pharisees and Sadducees—religious leaders of the Jews—as well as the Jewish people themselves toward Samaritans, Moabites, and others. Then Jesus came along and upsets the order of things when he suggested we are to love our neighbor whoever they may be and also to pray for those who persecute us.

Liberation Theology suggests we read the Bible through the lens of those on the margins of society rather than those of religious leaders and others in authority. The Gospel narrative is driven around a conflict of values; Jesus set his teaching over against the religious and political leaders of the time (who stood for the status quo). He was in conflict with those benefiting from the current political and social system. Jesus was leading a movement in response to the Roman Empire and the powerful ones of his day. It began as a renewal movement within Judaism known as "the Way" that appealed to the marginalized of society, those whom the political system oppressed. Jesus offered a vision of a flourishing life in the midst of oppression and taught alternative practices that could lead to an alternative and more hopeful reality.

The story of Jesus and the Gerasene Demonic in the Gospel of Luke offers an example of his willingness to challenge the systemic issues of his day:

Then they arrived at the country of the Gerasenes, which is opposite Galilee. And when he [Jesus] had stepped out on land; a man of the city who had demons met him. For a long time he had worn no clothes, and he did not live in a house but in the tombs. When he saw Jesus, he fell down before him and shouted at the top of his voice, "What have you to do with me, Jesus, Son of the Most High God? I beg you, do not torment me."—for Jesus had commanded the unclean spirit to come out of the man. (For many times it had seized him; he was kept under guard and bound with chains and shackles, but he would break the bonds and be driven by the demon into the wilds.) Jesus then asked him, "What is your name?" He said, "Legion"; for many demons had entered him. They begged him not to order them to go back into the abyss.

Now there on the hillside a large herd of swine was feeding; and the demons begged Jesus to let them enter these. So he gave them permission. Then the demons came out of the man and entered the swine, and the herd rushed down the steep bank into the lake and was drowned.

When the swineherds saw what had happened, they ran off and told it in the city and in the country. Then people came out to see what it was that had happened, and when they came to Jesus, they found the man from whom the demons had gone sitting at the feet of Jesus, clothed and in his right mind. And they were afraid. Those who had seen it told them how the one possessed by demons had been healed. Then all the people of the surrounding country of the Gerasenes asked Jesus to leave them; for they were seized with great fear. (Luke 8:26–37)

Luke was not simply telling another healing miracle of Jesus. The story is also an allegory meant to relate a greater truth, one of liberation from the powers and prejudices that oppress people and hold them captive. The demon-possessed man who had been chained up in a cave may represent all who were being oppressed by the Roman government in that time. Legion, the name of the demon, could have a double meaning as well. It may represent the Roman legion of soldiers who kept the people of Palestine restrained and in line. It could also refer to the many who were constrained by their own reli- gious and cultural prejudices. Note the reaction of the crowd when they real- ized the man had been healed and made whole. They asked Jesus to leave because he had disturbed the status quo. Jesus, like Atticus Finch, held up a mirror to society, and they didn't like what they saw. Jesus and Atticus are both truth-tellers seeking to usher in nothing less than a new world order, one that is fair and just for all.

When viewed through the lens of the marginalized—the poor, the outcast, and the oppressed—this Bible text reveals as much about the flawed culture of the day as it does about the man at the center of the story. It turns out that he, like the Black defendant Tom Robinson in *To Kill a Mockingbird,* was really a scapegoat. Each man may have been possessed by demons of some kind, which are not necessarily of their own making; for they each seem to bear the blame for all that was wrong or evil in their respective communities. Luke has revealed a defect in the system that makes certain people—usually those on the margin—a scapegoats for the rest of society. Instead of being able to admit one's own shortcomings, it is easier to blame others—especially those considered lower on the food chain. And the real sin of arrogance is when those at the top of society—the rich, the powerful, and the privileged of any culture—dismiss or look down on those they do not believe to be as worthy as themselves.

From Arrogance to Humility

The Prophet Micah reminds us to "walk humbly with God" (Micah 6:8). This implies that we approach not only God but one another with a sense of humility and vulnerability. As individuals and as a culture, we must learn to put our arrogance and sense of superiority aside if real and transformative change is to take place. There cannot be change without some degree of vulnerability, which implies uncertainty, risk-taking, emotional exposure, and a sense of openness. One cannot be vulnerable from a state of arrogance where we place our own power, safety, and comfort first. For those of the Christian persuasion, the person of Jesus Christ can be an example:

> Let the same mind be in you that was in Christ Jesus, who though he was in the form of God, did not regard equality with God as something to be exploited, but emptied himself, taking the form of a slave, being born in human likeness. And being found in human form, he humbled himself and became obedient to the point of death—even death on a cross. (*Philippians 2:5–8*)

The First Step of Humility

The first step is to *bear witness to the truth* and to admit our own failings as a nation. That may seem counter intuitive to many politicians and religious leaders of our day. Yet rather than colluding with the "Empire" as it has in the past, the church today has a prophetic role to be a truth-teller. It can recount the sordid history of how those who settled this country exploited the land and enslaved its people. An example of this was a public declaration made by the Seattle Council of Churches in 1988 "To the Tribal Councils and Traditional Spiritual Leaders of the Indian and Eskimo Peoples of the Pacific Northwest":

Dear Brothers and Sisters,

This is a formal apology on behalf of our churches for their long-standing participation in the destruction of traditional Native American spiritual practices. We call upon our people for recognition of and respect for your traditional ways of life and for protection of your sacred places and ceremonial objects. We have frequently been unconscious and insensitive and have not come to your aid when you have been victimized by unjust Federal policies and practices. In many other circumstances we reflected the rampant racism and prejudice of the dominant culture with which we too willingly identified. During the 200th Anniversary year of the United States Constitution we, as leaders of our churches in the Pacific Northwest, extend our apology. We ask for your forgiveness and blessing.

As the Creator continues to renew the earth, the plants, the animals and all living things, we call upon the people of our denominations and fellowship to a commitment of mutual support in your efforts to reclaim and protect the legacy of your own traditional spiritual teachings. . . . May the God of Abraham and Sarah, and the Spirit who lives in both the cedar and Salmon People be honored and celebrated.[5]

The anti-Jewish sentiment and rise in violence against the Jewish community in this country and elsewhere has already been noted. Here again, the Christian church and other communities of faith can acknowledge their complicity in fanning the flames of prejudice and hatred. In an effort to do just that, the Church Council of the Evangelical Lutheran Church in America adopted a document in 1994 as a statement on Lutheran-Jewish relations:

In the long history of Christianity there exists no more tragic development accorded the Jewish people on the part of Christian believers. Very few Christian communities of faith were able to escape the contagion of anti-Judaism and its modern successor, anti-Semitism. Lutherans belonging to the Lutheran World Federation and the Evangelical

Lutheran Church in America feel a special burden in this regard because of certain elements in the legacy of the reformer Martin Luther and the catastrophes, including the Holocaust of the twentieth century, suffered by Jews in places where the Lutheran churches were strongly represented . . .

Grieving the complicity of our own tradition within this history of hatred, moreover, we express our urgent desire to live out our faith in Jesus Christ with love and respect for the Jewish people. We recognize in anti-Semitism a contradiction and an affront to the Gospel, a violation of our hope and calling, and we pledge this church to oppose the deadly working of such bigotry, both within our own circles and in the society around us. Finally, we pray for the continued blessing of the Blessed One upon the increasing cooperation and understanding between Lutheran Christians and Jews.[6]

The Evangelical Lutheran Church in America, perhaps one of the whitest denominations in the country, took bold steps at their 2019 churchwide assembly in Milwaukee, Wisconsin, to address the issues of racism and white supremacy. Actions included a resolution condemning white supremacy and racist rhetoric as well as a public apology titled "Declaration of the ELCA to People of African Descent." According to Presiding Bishop Elizabeth Eaton, "In the context of the quadricentennial remembrance of American slavery in this country, we acknowledge that racism and white supremacy are deeply rooted in that history, and that the church is complicit. This apology means working toward a deeper understanding of slavery and its legacy, of institutional and structural racism, of white privilege, and of attitudes and foundations of white supremacy . . . so we may be better equipped to speak boldly about the equal dignity of all persons in the eyes of God."[7] (See Appendix 3 for full text.) While celebrating cultural, ethnic, and racial diversity, the ELCA committed itself to confront racism of all kinds and to advocate for justice and fairness for all people. It also acknowledged that it is a church that belongs to Christ, where there is a place for everyone.

Likewise, the Christian Church (Disciples of Christ) at their 2017 General Assembly in Des Moines adopted a resolution that called for a new "Poor People's Campaign: A National Call for Moral Revival." This effort, based on Rev. Dr. Martin Luther King Jr.'s original campaign fifty years ago, established the Poor People's Moral Action Congress held in June 2019. Activities included release of a Moral Budget, a forum with presidential candidates, and a Freedom School for church leaders.

Repentance, Redemption, and Reconciliation

There are numerous models of truth-telling, and perhaps the most well-known is the *Truth and Reconciliation Commission* established by South African President Nelson Mandela in the aftermath of apartheid. Mandela knew that his country was deeply divided and on the verge of a civil war between the Native Africans and the white citizens of European descent. For years, the white colonialists had wielded oppressive power over their African neighbors. Following his election as the first black president of the country, he asked Anglican Archbishop Desmond Tutu to establish a reconciliation process that would help heal the deep wounds that remained.

The process involved having the victims of apartheid meet with their oppressors, those who committed acts of violence against them. In the first phase, someone who had been brutally beaten or a parent whose child had been murdered would meet with the perpetrator. The one who had caused harm would have to listen to the story of how they had harmed another—often hearing the cries of pain and anguish of their victim. The offender was next offered a chance to apologize and make amends. The injured party was then afforded an opportunity to decide the fate of the accused, even to offer forgiveness and seek reconciliation.

The Second Step of Humility

A second step of genuine humility is that of *repentance and forgiveness.* Every person has a need to forgive and to be forgiven. In *The Book of Forgiving: The Four-Fold Path for Healing Ourselves and Our World*, Desmond Tutu drew from the lessons he learned while leading the Truth and Reconciliation Commission in South Africa. He described four steps to healing: (1) admitting the wrong and acknowledging the harm; (2) telling one's story and witnessing the anguish; (3) asking forgiveness and granting forgiveness; and (4) renewing or releasing the relationship. Although forgiveness is hard work, Tutu believed that it is only through this four-fold path that one can be free of the endless and unyielding cycle of pain and retribution that afflicts so many people and communities.[8]

Other nations have chosen to take such a course of action. Similar to the United States, Canada was founded on colonial genocidal policies—that guided the way it treated the First Nations people—even to the point of genocide. According to the United Nation's 1948 definition, genocide is any of five acts committed with the "intent to destroy in whole or in part, a national, ethnical, racial, or religious group." These acts include: (a) killing members of a particular group; (b) causing serious bodily or mental harm to members of the group; (c) deliberately inflicting on the group conditions of life calculated to bring about its physical destruction in whole or in part; (d) imposing measures intended to prevent births within the group; and (e) forcibly transferring children of the group to another group.[9]

Several religious organizations including the Anglican Church of Canada encouraged and assisted the government of Canada in establishingt the Truth and Reconciliation Commission of Canada in 2008.[10] The Commission spent six years traveling to all parts of Canada and heard from more than sixty-five hundred witnesses. The Commission also hosted national events and sought to educate people across Canada on the need to develop respectful and just relationships between Indigenous people and Canada.[11] *A Litany of Repentance and Reconciliation* was crafted by the Evangelical Lutheran Church in Canada for their national assembly in the summer of 2019 and can be found in Appendix 2 of this book.

The Uniting Church of Australia recently sought to help heal past wounds of the nation—created by atrocities inflicted on its Indigenous Peoples—by declaring a national "Day of Mourning" on Sunday, January 20, 2019. It was meant to be observed concurrently with Australia Day, which commemorates the arrival of the First Fleet from England on January 25, 1788 and the 150th anniversary of the United Aboriginal Day of Mourning first observed on January 26, 1938. The event was meant to bring to light and encourage repentance for the willful disregard for the past pain and suffering of the First Nation or Indigenous people of Australia by the European colonists over many years. Leading up to the "Day of Mourning" the Uniting Church of Australia made a covenant with the United Aboriginal and Islander Christian Conference and prepared a liturgy of repentance and reconciliation to be used in all of its congregations. (See Appendix 1.)

Another example of humility was the 2020 landmark decision of the California Assembly to apologize to Japanese Americans for their interment during World War II. Recognizing the forced removal of more than 120,000 Americans of Japanese descent from their homes and businesses, the bill spelled out in excruciating detail the state's anti-Japanese heritage including the 1943 joint resolution by the California Assembly and state Senate calling for the forfeiture of US citizenship by residents who were also residents of Japan. The 2020 bill, authored by Assemblyman Al Muratsuchi, sought to connect history with the present political climate. "Given recent national events," it states, "it is all the more important to learn from the mistakes of the past and to ensure that such an assault on freedom will never again happen to any community in the United States."[12]

The state of California provides an example of repentance and reconciliation for the rest of the nation in its previous actions as well. In 2006, the state formally apologized for the California Senate's role in the forced repatriation of more than 1 million Mexican immigrants—many of them American citizens—to Mexico during the Great Depression, and in 2009 it repented for the 1882 Chinese Exclusion Act that banned Chinese immigration for more than sixty years. And in 2019, Governor Gavin Newson signed an executive order formally apologizing for the state's mistreatment of Native Americans throughout history, even to the point of acknowledging it as genocide.

The Future of America Is One that Celebrates Many Faiths and Cultures

Indonesian Americans of different faith backgrounds who lived in the Greater Seattle area came together in the spring of 2019 seeking reconciliation. They were acutely aware that in Indonesia those of the Christian tradition and Muslim faith view each other with suspicion, enmity, and often hatred. Indonesian immigrants and their families desired a different way, especially in the aftermath of the mass murder of Christians in Sri Lanka by Islamic terrorists. Muslims and Christians sat down together to share their fears and hopes. They listened to one another's stories and they sought common ground. Because both faiths came out of the Abrahamic tradition, they discovered they had similar values and a desire to be in relationship with each other. They developed a covenant of reconciliation and understanding to lead them forward into a new era of mutual respect.

The Third Step of Humility

The example above describes a third step of humility: a willingness to put one's own preconceived notions and bias aside, to listen and learn from one another, with the goal being that of *establishing mutual respect.*

Saint Paul reminds us that God seeks to break down the barriers that separate us when he writes in his Letter to the Galatians, "You are all children of God through faith. . . . There is no longer Jew or Greek, there is no longer slave or free, there is no longer male and female, for all of you are one in Christ Jesus" (Galatians 3:26–28).

This was a radical message for a world that divided people by multiple categories. In his seminal work, *The Forgotten Creed: Christianity's Original*

Struggle Bigotry, Slavery, and Sexism, theologian Stephen J. Patterson suggests that Paul has actually borrowed his text from an earlier baptismal creed used by the early church, perhaps one of the oldest statements of faith made in the New Testament. It was to signify the kind of community into which the newly baptized were being initiated. It was an egalitarian community that celebrated inclusion, diversity, and equality. Patterson writes, "It is surprising that people have been thinking about race, class, and gender for a very long time, and the followers of Jesus in fact were trying to undermine these pernicious gauges of human worth right from the beginning."[13]

This early creed suggests that such categories as Jew or Greek, slave and free, male and female are all false distinctions that have no basis in God's reality. Addressing the human divide today, we might add that there is no longer Christian or Muslim, black or white, gay or straight, rich or poor. The Indonesian community in Seattle—both Muslim and Christian—demonstrated they had learned the truth that they were equally children of God and they should not let differences of belief or practice separate them any longer.

It seems fair to say—for multiple reasons—that the future of America is not going to be that of a Christian nation. It is a myth that America was founded on Christian principles when the leaders of the Continental Congress were rather influenced by the Enlightenment and such secular writers as Voltaire and Rousseau. It is also dubious to suggest that God has a preference for America over other nations or has destined it—the United States to be primarily a Christian nation going forward. We have cited the fact that only about 50 percent of the US population claim to be members of the Christian faith, and that number is in decline. We also recognize that America continues to be a nation of immigrants who bring a variety of religions and cultures with them. It is the height of arrogance for a once-dominant majority (Christian) to disrespect or despise those who are of another faith or no faith. Rather we must find a way to respect one another, celebrate our diversity, and work together for the common good.

When he was crowned emperor of France in 1804, Napoleon Bonaparte said there could be no future for France as only a Catholic nation. France had a history of persecuting both Protestants and Jews, and many non-Catholics had been driven out of the country such as when the Huguenots were expelled. Napoleon recognized the arrogance and folly of this. He saw the value of all French citizens—regardless of religion or culture—working together to build a stronger nation. And where Protestants and Jews had been forbidden to worship publicly, but he proposed establishing houses of worship—churches and synagogues—for those who were not of the Catholic faith.

Likewise, there can be no future for America as solely a Christian nation. We must learn to embrace a diversity of ethnic, cultural, and faith traditions if we are to grow and flourish as a nation. Recognizing that we already live in a post-Christian era, we can be free to celebrate the freedom of religion we have in this country without any one religion forcing its beliefs on another. We can respect one another despite our differences and find ways to work together to make an impact for good in our communities. Together we can seek and work for that which brings healing and wholeness to our nation and to our world: diversity, equity, and justice.

The world is a conflict-ridden zone. Yet there are glimpses of hope around the globe as women and men unite to overcome divisions and heal the wounds of the past. The following hymn based on Micah 6:8 suggests a way forward for America and the rest of the planet:

> *Come, open your heart! Show your mercy to all those in fear!*
> *We are called to be hope for the hopeless so hatred and*
>   *blindness will be no more.*
> *We are called to act with justice, we are called to love tenderly.*
> *We are called to serve one another, to walk humbly with God.*[14]

Questions for Reflection

1. What issues or truths are common in the story of the Gerasene Demonic (Luke 8:26–39) and in *To Kill a Mockingbird*?

2. How would you describe the "sin of arrogance"?

3. Why does humility require a degree of vulnerability?

4. What are three of the steps or examples of humility described in this chapter.

5. Consider some of the examples of repentance and reconciliation mentioned in this chapter. Which one do you think best describes "walking humbly with God"?

5

Values Matter

Discovering Common Values in Many Faith Traditions

You cannot reap what you have not sown. How are
we going to reap LOVE in our community, if we
only sow HATE?

—Oscar Romero

What are the Core Values that shape life together? Are there shared values that we can point to by which we might forge a new future as a nation and a world? People from different faith traditions may discover they have more in common than they at first realize. At the Dayton International Peace Museum, there is the *Golden Rule Room* that contains displays of inter-religious cooperation in the city of Dayton, Ohio. It is so named because of a "Peace Labyrinth" quilt designed by artist Janet McTavish. In her tapestry, she sought to show that love and the Golden Rule are common threads found in all of the world's religions, although expressed in different ways. In Buddhism we read: "Hurt not others with that which pains yourself." In Christianity, "Do unto others as you would have them do unto you." In Hinduism, "Treat others as you would yourself be treat." In Islam, "Do unto all men as you would wish to have done unto you." In Judaism, "What you yourself hate, do to no man." In Native American, "Live in harmony, for we are all related." And in Sacred Earth, "Do as you will, as long as you harm no one."[1] This chapter explores some common values found in a variety of religious traditions.

The Jewish Way

It is said there is nothing new under the sun. About seven hundred years before Jesus of Nazareth was crucified for his radical public criticism of the oppressive Roman and Judean political, economic, and religious domination systems of their time, the Hebrew prophets railed a critique of the oppressive power structures of their day. Standing somewhere in Samaria, the capital of the norther Israelite Kingdom, the Prophet Amos shouted to anyone who would listen:

> I hate, I despise your festivals
>> and I take no pleasure in your solemn assemblies.
> Even though you offer me your burnt offerings and grain offerings,
>> I will not accept them;
>> and the offerings of your fatted animals
>> I will not look upon.
> Take away from me the noise of your songs;
>> I will not listen to the melody of your harps.
> But let justice roll down like waters,
>> And righteousness [solidarity of community] like an ever-flowing
>> stream. (Amos 5:21–26)

And a few years later, the prophet Micah would proclaim from Jerusalem:

> With what shall I come before the Lord
>> and bow myself before God on high?
> Shall I come before him with burnt offerings
>> with calves a year old?
> Will the Lord be pleased with thousands of rams
>> with ten rivers of oil?
> Shall I give the firstborn for my transgression,
>> the fruit of my body for the sin of my soul?
> He has told you, O mortal, what is good:
>> and what the Lord requires of you
> but to do justice and to love kindness,
>> and to walk in solidarity of community with God. (Micah 6:6–8)[2]

Each of the eighth-, seventh-, and sixth-century BCE prophets whose oracles are preserved in the Tanach[3] stood squarely within the Exodus tradition of God's covenant with Israel, a covenant requiring the creation of community rooted in justice and compassion so as to be a "light to the nations," as Deutero-Isaiah put it—an example of solidarity of community for other societies to imitate in their own distinctive ways. Everything else—religious obligations and practices, legal obligations, political loyalties, economic and social hierarchies, and power structures—are less than of secondary importance. In particular, religious teachings and practices must not be used as ideological cover-ups to justify injustice and violence.

In Hebrew, the word translated into English as "justice" is *mišpat* or "right treatment of human beings," which according to the biblical prophets depended upon creating communal structures upon which human beings can depend for peaceful communities, which too often is not what human beings actually experience. "Justice" means giving all people what they need for meaningful existence, which oftentimes is not what people want.

The nondual side of *mišpat* is *hesed* or "compassion." "Compassion" is the experience of a person or community suffering injustice and then relating justly by resisting personal and institutional forms of injustice. This in turn is the foundation of *śedaqah*, which is usually translated as "righteousness." But "righteousness" does not adequately convey the nuances of *śedaqah*. A more accurate translation is "solidarity of community," which from the second century BCE until the present was imagined by the prophets remembered in the Tanach and the writers of the New Testament as a "commonwealth of God" finally established by God with the appearance of a Messiah, an "Anointed One."[4]

As noted, the English word for *hesed*, is "compassion." Literally, "compassion" means "to suffer with," and it occurs when we experience the suffering of other human beings and sentient beings as our own and attempt to relieve this suffering because it *is* our own. The English noun "compassion" derives from Latin. Its first syllable derives from *cum*, meaning "with." The "passion" of "compassion" is derived from *passus*, which is the past participle of the verbs *patior, pati, passus*, and *passus sum*. "Compassion" is thus related to the English word "patient" ("one who suffers"), from *patiens*, and is akin to the Greek verb *paskhein* ("to suffer") and to its cognate noun *pathos*.

But "compassion" does not merely name a subjective feeling in response to suffering. This is so because "compassion" is grounded in the utter interdependency of all things and events, apart from which there would exist no things or events, because of God's continuing creation of the world. This means that all human and nonhuman beings are "relatives," part of an extended family that included all life forms sharing planet Earth. Accordingly, "compassion," ontologically grounded in interdependence, is what happens when we wake up to the fact that we and all life forms dwell in a world in which no thing or event is separate from any other thing or event. In other words, we have never been, nor are we now, separate beings. The suffering of others as well as the suffering of all living beings with whom we share life on this planet *is our own suffering.*

This is one of the reasons we have long thought that the story of Jacob's combat with God at the River Jabbok is the major paradigm encompassing the journey of faith for Jews, Christians, and Muslims.[5] For Jews, wrestling with God requires following God's "instructions" in the Torah to create just, compassionate structures of communal existence. It has more often than not been a bruising experience throughout Jewish history. For wrestling with God requires faith—meaning "trust," not "belief in doctrines"—that requires betting one's life on something; in Jacob's case, on the reality of what he encountered in his wrestling match with God. For Jews, Christians, and Muslims, "faith" is God's way of starting a fight with us. A hip—or something else—will be thrown out of joint—and we will limp, like Jacob, throughout the remainder of our lives.

As the history of Jewish experience records, wrestling with God's demand that human beings establish just, compassionate communal structures always leave faithful Jews with scars. "Being Jewish" *means* participating in a communal effort to establish compassionate, just communal structures for the common good. This is the heart of God's Torah ("instructions"). It was for this that Jews have been "chosen," so as to be "light to the nations," as Deutero Isaiah put it (49:6). But it's one thing for a community to be *called* to live justly and compassionately; it's quite another thing to figure out *how* to create communal structures of existence that are actually compassionate and just. So in imitation of limping Jacob, whom God renamed "Israel," meaning "he who wrestles with God and wins," Jewish experience is a never-ending history of wrestling with God to figure out *how* to live in accordance with the Torah's instructions throughout the ever-shifting conditions of Jewish history.

The Christian Way

The prophetic demand for justice, compassion, and solidarity of community was the heart of the teachings of the historical Jesus. This is not surprising, since he was a first-century CE Israelite whose teachings were grounded in the prophetic traditions preserved in his day. Accordingly, the New Testament's word, *agape* or "love," to describe Jesus's teachings is not the Hebrew or Aramaic word he would have employed. As a first century Israelite, he used the word *hesid.* "Love" in biblical Hebrew (*āhavah*) has strong erotic connotations absent from the prophetic understanding of compassion that was the center of Jesus's teachings and actions.

Most Jesus scholars agree that Jesus was both a mystic and a political activist. Like most mystics, he experienced both apophatic experiences of union with God (experiences indescribable with words, which cannot describe the fullness of God) and kataphatic experiences of God's continual presence (experiences of God describable in words). As a teacher of wisdom—a "sage" as wisdom teachers are commonly called—and like the biblical prophets before him, he publicly criticized the unjust power structures of his day. Compassion, justice, and solidarity of community were the topics of all of his authentic aphorisms and parables preserved in the Synoptic Gospels.

But there are two types of wisdom, which means here are two types of sages. The most common wisdom is conventional wisdom, and its teachers are conventional sages. Conventional wisdom is "what everyone knows," a culture's collective understanding about what is real and how to live in accordance with what is real. The second type of wisdom is an alternative; it is subversive wisdom that undermines conventional wisdom and points to an alternative path or "way of life." Its teachers are subversive sages. For example, the historical Buddha and the Daoist sage Zhuangzi taught "Ways" that lead away from conventional values toward a way of life that reflects "the way things really are." The wisdom of subversive sages is the wisdom of "the road less traveled," whose distinguishing character was described by the thirteenth century Christian mystic Maguerite Porete as "living without a why."[6]

It is well established that Jesus, like the prophets before him, was an oral teacher who employed aphorisms and parables. Aphorisms are short, easy-to-remember sayings, like great one-liners. Parables are essentially short stories. Together, the aphorisms and parables preserved in the Synoptic Gospels place us directly in contact with the voice of the historical Jesus because according to contemporary Jesus scholarship, the most certain thing we know about Jesus, because he lived in a culture in which literacy rates were quite low, is that he was a storyteller and a speaker of great one-liners. Jesus's aphorisms and parables are invitational forms of speech. He used them to invite his hearers to apprehend something they might not have otherwise apprehended. Aphorisms and parables tease the imagination into action by suggesting more than they directly say and invite a transformation of perception and understanding. In many ways, they function like *kōans* in Zen Buddhist meditational practices.

Jesus spoke of "the narrow way" that leads to life and subverts "the broad way" followed by conventional human beings, which leads to injustice and death. Jesus's aphorisms are crystallizations that invite further reflection as they generate startling insights. "You cannot serve two masters"; "You cannot get grapes from a bramble bush"; "If a blind person leads a blind person, will they not both fall into a ditch?"; "Leave the dead to bury the dead"; "You strain out gnat and wallow a camel. These are all are short, provocative one-liners that say more than their literal meanings as they invite hearers to apprehend something they might not otherwise understand.[7]

Some of the parables are very short, as brief as a typical aphorism. His short parables are memorable, enigmatic sayings complete in themselves. For example:

To what should I compare the Kingdom (Commonwealth) of God? It is like yeast that a woman took and mixed with three measures of flour until all of it was leavened. (Luke 13:20–21 = Matthew 13:33)

The kingdom of heaven is like treasure hidden in a field, which someone found and hid; then in his joy he goes and sells all that he has and buys that field. (Matthew 13:44)

But most of Jesus's recorded parables are similar to short stories with plot and character development. It is probable that Jesus would have told them numerous times in different ways and may have expanded them to different lengths depending on his audience.

Jesus employed aphorisms and parables to subvert conventional wisdom and replace it with subversive wisdom. Conventional wisdom is the dominant wisdom of any culture, a culture's most taken-for-granted communal understanding about the way things are and how to live in harmony with the way things are. Conventional wisdom, in other words, summarizes a culture's dominant worldview, a culture's social construction of reality and the internalization of that structure within the psyche of individuals. These conventional social constructions of reality are opposed to the prophetic call for just, compassionate community.

Moreover, conventional wisdom is supported by institutionalized systems of rewards and punishments: you reap what you sow; follow this way, and all will be well; you receive what you deserve; the righteous will prosper—these are the examples of the constant messages of conventional wisdom. Socially, conventional wisdom creates a world of hierarchies and boundaries. Some of these are inherited, exemplified when differences in gender, race, or physical condition are given hierarchical value and social roles. Politically, conventional wisdom is the ideological foundation of oppressive social, political, and economic systems of institutionalized systems of unjust oppression.

But the conflict between the ways of conventional and subversive wisdom is not only part of the histories of the Jewish and Christian Ways. For the subversive wisdom of the world's religious Ways affirms justice and compassion as the foundations of solidarity of community in their own distinctive ways as the means for resisting oppressive individual and communal structures of existence. The struggle against unjust domination systems is on-going and crosses religious boundaries and continues to this day. There is great diversity in how various religious ways have reflected on the interdependence of justice, compassion, and solidarity of community. But there are also similarities. The similarities and differences are points for entering a socially engaged interreligious dialogue as a means of establishing solidarity of community for the common good in an interdependent world.

There also exists a hard truth: resisting injustice is one thing; establishing just communal systems founded on justice and compassion remains an unrealized goal in spite of a minority human response to the prophetic call to resistance. Communal systems of justice and community remain a perpetual ideal to be pursued but perhaps never fully realized in the rough-and-tumble of life—which does not mean that we should avoid taking the road less traveled in the struggle for compassionate community.

This is certainly the view of 2 Corinthians, in which Paul describes God as the "Father of Compassion" and the "God of all comfort":

> Blessed be the God and Father of our Lord Jesus Christ, the Father of mercies and the God of all consolation, who consoles us in our afflictions, so that we may be able to console those who are in any affliction with the consolation with which we ourselves are consoled by God. For just as the sufferings of Christ are abundant for us, so also our consolation is abundant through Christ. If we are being afflicted, it is for your consolation and salvation; if we are comforted, it is for your comfort and salvation; if we are being consoled, it is for your consolation, which you experience when you patiently endure the same suffering that we are also suffering. Our hope for you is unshaken, for we know that as you share in our sufferings, so also you share in our consolation. (2 Corinthians 1:3–7)

So, for Christians, the historical Jesus declared to be the Christ of faith embodies the model of compassionate justice according to which human relationships should be constructed in solidarity of community. Justice and compassion, as the parable of the Good Samaritan holds up, should be extended to all human beings, including one's enemies.[8]

The Islamic Way

"Justice" and "compassion" are the most frequently occurring words in the Qur'an. Furthermore, each of its 114 chapters, with the exception of the ninth chapter, begins with the invocation, "In the name of God, the

Compassionate, the Merciful. . . . " The Arabic word for "compassion" is *rahman. Namaz*, or daily prayer five times per day that is one of the "Five Pillars" by which the Qur'an defines the practice of *Islām* ("surrender to God's will"), begins by invoking "Allah, the Merciful and Compassionate." "Compassion" and "the Just" are two of the "Ninety-nine Beautiful Names of God."

As in Jewish teaching and Christian mystical teaching, "compassion" is what human beings experience when they become aware of God's creation of the universe that conjoins all things and events into a web of mutual interdependence and are thereby moved to live justly. Thus, another human being's suffering is, in part, one's own since all human beings are brothers and sisters no matter what religious label one chooses to wear or not wear. Compassion and justice create a relationship in which one actively works to relieve non-compassion and injustice in whatever forms they occur in human community in general, referred to by the Qur'an as the "House of Islam" (*dar al-islām*). And those who don't live by justice and compassion are not included in the "House of Islam." The heart of justice, compassion, and Islam is the principle of *tawhid, or the* "oneness" or "unity" of God. This unity is intrinsically linked to Islamic teaching of the interdependence of compassion, justice, and community. Thus, "My mercy encompasses all things" (Qur'an 7:156). Accordingly, the Qur'an identifies sentiments like loving compassion as an expression of the interconnected unity of all human beings that reflects the oneness and unity of God.

The Qur'an frequently speaks of God's plan for diversity, and the goodness of diversity as an ingredient in God's and humanity's "unity." For example,

O mankind, we have indeed created you male and female, and made you as nations and tribes that you may come to know one another. (49:13)

And every community has its direction of which He lets them turn towards it. Vie, therefore, with one another in doing good works. Wherever you may be God will gather you all unto him. (2:148)

There is no compulsion in religion. (2:256)

Truly, those who believe, and the Jews and the Christians and Sabeans—whoever believes in God and the Day of Judgement and act virtuously will receive their reward from their Lord; no fear or grief will befall them. (2:62)

Whoever saves the life of one human being, it shall be as if he had saved the whole of human kind. (5:32)

The great mystical writers of Islam, the Sufis, wrote constantly of justice and compassion as essential to the practice of Islam. They described compassion as the remedy for all ills and the alchemy of existence; compassion transforms poverty into riches, war into peace, ignorance into knowledge, and hell into paradise. For example, Jalal al-Din Rumi, who was born in modern-day Afghanistan in 1207 CE, is arguably the best known of all Sufi mystics. He wrote that while compassion is the foundation of the Sufi Way, it is a reality that can only be known by experience in order to be truly understood. In his words, "Love [Compassion] cannot be contained within our speaking and listening. It is an ocean whose depths cannot be plumbed. . . . Love [Compassion] cannot be found in erudition and science, books and pages. . . . The kernel of Love [Compassion] is a mystery that cannot be resolved."[9]

The Sufis in their own individual poetic languages understood that the compassionate character love entails embracing diversity, or what we call today, "pluralism," rooted in the experience of transcendence of self. Transcendence of self—that is, of the illusion that we exist in separation from other human beings, God, and the life forms with which we share planet Earth—is not the only source of Sufi spirituality. For example, Abu Bakr Muhammed Ibn al Arabi (1165–1240 CE), who was born in the Andalusia region of Spain, is one of the greatest writers in the Islamic mystical tradition. Known as the poet of the "Cosmic Heart," he wrote "Discovering the Deeper Grounds of Suffering in Opening the Heart." In it, he wrote, "Thus the person who understands the meaning of suffering increases his loving compassion for the one who is in pain will be rewarded. . . . " because "as the Arab proverb expresses it, 'every moist heart is a divine reward.'"[10]

The Hindu Way

What non-Hindus name "Hinduism" is an abstraction from what Hindus who practice the Hindu Way actually do and experience. That is, the label "Hinduism" covers a religious tradition in which every idea, practice, and myth that has ever occurred in human imagination can be found in some form in the Hindu Way. Of course, pluralism is an ingredient in all religious Ways. Just how many ways are there of being Jewish? Or Christian? Or Muslim? But unlike the pluralism of Christian tradition, Jewish faith and practice, Islam, the Buddhist tradition, or the Daoist and Confucian cumulative traditions, there exists no defining teaching or practice characterizing the pluralism of "Hinduism" to which all Hindus assent. This being said, justice and compassion are virtues having many shades of meaning in the classical texts of the Hindu Way, meanings that center on the word *darsán* or "seeing" or "apprehension."

Once upon a time, the God Śiva and the goddess Pārvati were sporting in their high Himalayan home when Pārvati covered Śiva's eyes with her hands. The whole universe was plunged into darkness. For when Śiva's eyes are closed the whole universe was plunged into darkness, except for the fire of his third eye that always threatens the destruction of the world. The all-seeing gods are said to never close their eyes, and from the near disaster of Śiva's and Pārvati's play, it's clearly a good thing they do not, because our well-being is dependent on the open eyes of the gods.

So according to the Hindu Way, not only must the gods keep their eyes open, so must we in order to make contact with them, to reap their blessings, and to know their secrets. When followers of the Hindu Way go to a temple, their eyes meet the powerful, eternal gaze of a deity, often many deities. It is called *darsán*, "seeing" the gods as they really are, without "delusion," or *māyā*. The traditions of the Hindu Way are all an attempt to "see" Brahman— of which the numerous deities of Hindu tradition are limited "incarnations" or *avatars*—without delusion so as to live without delusion. Thus, if there is a single thread uniting the Hindu Way, it is *darsán*. For "reality," meaning "the way things really are," can be apprehended at all times and all places—if we know how to look. The Hindu Way is a pluralism of ways of training human beings how to apprehend this reality, usually named "Brahman" or "Sacred Power" that is "in with, and under" the particular things and events of existence.

One can understand that the plurality of Hindu teachings and practices are methods of training persons to apprehend by experience that all things and events are self-expressions (*ātman*) of Brahman; we must not confuse Brahman (sacred power) with our ego-self (*jīva*) or our sense of "I" as distinguished from other selves or other things and events. Absolutizing one's ego-self in separation from other ego-selves constitutes a "delusion" (*maya*) that makes one or one's community selfish, unjust, and non-compassionate. In more Western terms, ontologically justice and compassion arise from awareness that nothing is ever separate from anyone or anything else. For realizing that another human being or sentient being's suffering is indeed our own suffering engenders just, compassionate action to help that person or sentient find release from suffering.

The Sanskrit word most often used for "compassion" is *karunā*, and all the ideals of Hindu Wisdom regarding justice and compassion can be summarized in one word: *ahimasā*, meaning "non-injury" or nonviolence. Knowing by experience that all life is interdependent is the subjective source of a just, compassionate mind, the external expression of which is nonviolent interaction with all human and non-human sentient beings with which we share life on planet Earth. Furthermore, compassionate nonviolence extends far beyond avoiding causing physical harm; it also involves not causing harm through speech or thought.

The best-known twentieth-century advocate of justice guided by compassionate nonviolence is probably Mahatma Gandhi. According to Gandhi, justice and compassion require nonviolence in mind, speech, and action toward any creature. Specifically, this means (1) in mind, not to think maliciously of others; (2) in speech, not to use foul language, and more than this, to use language in a disciplined way as a vehicle to communicate ideas and values relative to the abilities and mental capacities of one's hearers; and (3) in action to avoid actions that do injury to any person or creature or community of persons and creatures.

The Buddhist Way

Classical Buddhist approaches to justice and compassion begin with individual behavior and center on the Law of Karma, in which good actions generate positive consequences and bad actions negative consequences. For this reason, the Buddhist Way has proved historically compatible with any number of different political systems. Because the Buddhist Way has traditionally emphasized monastic life and discipline, Buddhist doctrine and practice have always focused on general social prescriptions, as exemplified by the "Five Precepts" of good conduct—not to injure any sentient being, not to lie, not to steal, not to commit immoral sexual acts, and not to partake of intoxicants—while acknowledging the existing political systems of the culture to which the Buddhist Way has been transmitted. In turn, rulers often patronized the *sangha*[11] ("community"), providing a mixture of protection and resources in return for the blessings of the monks and the wider political legitimacy their support afforded them.

These basic arrangements originated with King Ashoka on the Indian subcontinent in the third century BCE and continue through many contemporary democratic and autocratic regimes in Buddhist majority countries. The last two decades have witnessed the growth of movement cutting across all the major schools of the Buddhist Way called "Socially Engaged Buddhism," particularly in the United States, Europe, and Southeast Asia (Vietnam, Cambodia, and Myanmar), along with the support of the Dali Lama in his work to establish greater Tibetan autonomy from China.

The ultimate goal of a Buddhist practice is the attainment of Awakening, often described as "liberation" or *nirvanā*, and often interpreted as a state of being "extinguished," as in the extinguishing of a fire. Thus, *nirvanā* refers to the elimination or extinguishing of various mental and emotional or "defile-ments" that block an individual's attainment of Awakening—obstacles de-rived from the "poisons of desire for permanence, hatred, greed, and ignorance. In general, Mahayana Buddhist teaching about Awakening has a slightly broader meaning, referring to the attainment of "wisdom" (*prājñā*), which is interpreted as release from the recycling bondage of life and death.

Buddhist emphasis on individual Awakening is often portrayed as quietist. But historically, this is not an accurate characterization. Nevertheless, it is true that even today Buddhist teachers and philosophers rarely address social justice issues such as human rights, the just redistribution of resources, the impartial rule of law, and political freedom. Of course, the Buddhist Way is hardly alone in this regard. Almost all ancient philosophies and religious Ways paid scant at-tention to the interdependence of social justice. Even Catholicism, which ad-dressed social issues from early times in its history, did not concern itself with social justice issues or use this term in official documents until the latter part of the nineteenth century. Indeed, not until the eighteenth century did social jus-tice emerge as an important issue in political thought and social philosophy in the West. The last three centuries have thus seen the maturation of such key concepts a citizenship, political equality, and the fair distribution of economic resources. However, the process of modernization that drove the development of social philosophy in the West paradoxically retarded it in the East. Belatedly experiencing modernization as an experience of Western imperialism initiated by military and economic domination by Western colonial powers, Eastern in-tellectuals lost confidence in their native traditions, coming to see them as relics of the past without relevance to contemporary problems. As a result, indige-nous philosophies and religious Ways tended to be neglected in favor of the study of Western thought.

This process has only recently begun to reverse itself. As South and East Asian Buddhists became increasingly aware of the value of their particular cultural and religious identities, a new strain of Buddhist thought began to emerge, interested not only in relating the Buddhist Way to modern and postmodern concerns, but also in exploring the applicability of Buddhist no-tions of nonviolence to contemporary justice issues. Without doubt, the most important of these Buddhist groups is Socially Engaged Buddhism.

The term "socially engaged Buddhism" was first used as a description of contemporary traditions of Buddhist social activism by Sallie B. King in her analysis of Thich Nhất Hanh's notion "inner work," meaning the practice of meditation, and nonviolent "outer work," which King describes as "social en-gagement" with systemic structures of injustice.[12] Buddhist-Christian conceptual dialogue has generated deep interest in the relevance of dialogue for issues of social, environmental, economic, and gender justice.

Accordingly, socially engaged Buddhist-Christian dialogue is concerned with how Buddhists and Christians have mutually apprehended common experiences and resources for working together to help human beings liberate themselves and the environment from the global forces of systemic oppression.

Dialogue with Christian liberation theology has raised questions about the central role nonviolence has played in the Buddhist Way for twenty-five hundred years and whether Buddhists can develop their own distinctive understanding of justice. The key point is liberation theology's strong insistence on the interdependence of political, social, economic, and environmental justice, whereas traditional Buddhist teaching seems to have little to say about justice, in the sense that these teachings do not normally employ justice language. But there are well-known exceptions like B. R. Ambedkar and Sulak Sivaraksa, who never shy away from confronting justice issues as nonviolent Buddhists.

Of course, the question for all religious Ways is this: How exactly should the practice of nonviolence be related to the equally important requirement for justice in individual and communal relationships? This question is of particular importance for Buddhist faith and practice because of its stress on interdependent compassion, which seems to have little relevance to the violent injustice perpetrated on Cambodians murdered in the killing fields by oppressors claiming to be Buddhists. Sallie King, who is a practicing Zen Buddhist and Quaker, seeks a Buddhist "middle way" of joining the practice of nonviolence to the practice of justice. In a lecture given at the 2014 Annual Meeting of the Society for Buddhist Christian Studies, she explained:

> Looking at both the Buddhist and Christian ways of thinking, it seems that what we are dealing with here is a virtue with the characteristic of an Aristotelian mean. Let us call this virtue "critical voice." An *excessive* amount of "critical voice" is seen in strident, frequently angry self-righteous use of the prophetic voice and inability to hear the voice from the other side or a necessity to heat that side in order to resolve a situation. A *deficiency* of critical voice is seen in a failure to take on the prophetic voice when it is needed, a failure to criticize or condemn what should be condemned. It seems that engaged Buddhism tilts to the one side (the deficiency in critical voice) and needs to hear the correction from Liberation theology. Theology needs to tilt from the other side (the side of excessive critical voice) and needs to her the correction from engaged Buddhism.[13]

So here is the justice issue facing the Buddhist Way—a question that is not unique to the Buddhist Way. There has always existed in human history injustices so terrible, so destructive, so inhumane, so senseless, so deeply rooted in human nature that nonviolent compassion seems an irrelevant method of confrontation. Examples abound throughout human history, but the Killing Fields of Cambodia is one modern example. Confronting such collective evil requires the application of justice both to the perpetrators and those who survived collective violent oppression. Hopefully justice can be administered nonviolently with compassion, but more often than not justice is violent in its application, as described in Christian "just war" theory. The question for all religious Ways is this: exactly How should justice and compassion be balanced in confrontation with real issues of political, economic, and environmental injustice? For Buddhists, this question is particularly acute because there exists little interest in the concept of justice in the Buddhist world, with the exception of Socially Engaged Buddhism.

The Chinese Way

The religious history of China is incredibly complex and not reducible to separate strains of Daoist and Confucian tradition. Rather, it is more accurate to say that since the eighth century BCE the Chinese Way evolved from a blend of Daoist and Confucian strands into the Chinese Way, a Way of living in balanced harmony with nature within human Community. Accordingly, while the Daoist Way and the Confucian Way are utterly interdependent for most Chinese people, it will be necessary to treat each Way independently while keeping in mind that the Chinese way of seeking balanced harmony is with the polarities known as *yin* and *yang*.

One of the Daoist Ways most important concepts is *wu-wei*, the literal translation is "actionless-action," but "non-action" and "non-doing" are also employed as translations. But "actionless action" is in essence "action without attachment to the fruits of action." The classical symbol for *wu-wei* is free flowing water, as in a creek, river, or waterfall. As chapter 123 of the *Dao De Ching* (The Book of the Way and Its Virtue) describes it:

> Nothing under Heaven is softer or more yielding than water, but when it attacks hard and resistant things there is not one of them that prevail. For they can find no way of altering it. That the yielding conquers the resistant and soft conquers the hard is a fact known to human beings yet utilized by none.[14]

So "actionless action" is essentially the non-assertion of ego in action. That is, the classical Daoist tradition sought to train people through systems of meditation and physical disciplines to let go of all ego-centered desires in order to be naturally formed by the balancing process of nature. Thus, as we gradually learn to "do nothing" the Dao gradually does everything through us appropriate to our particular life situations. In the process, we gradually acquire *de* or "power," or more accurately "the power of virtue."

This means that for Daoists, *wu-wei* is the source for the practice of justice and compassion. *Yin* is an energy experienced as softness, yielding, going along with the ebbs and flows of natural process, as well as the energy sustaining compassion, while *yang, on the other hand,* is the energy of nature that is incarnated as hardness, resisting the flow of natural process, and, in human relationships, "justice." But according to both the Daoist and Confucian Ways, nature always seeks a balance between extreme expressions of *yin* and *yang.* Thus too much justice (*yang*) is a tyranny whereas too much *yin* is mere sentimentality irrelevant to the needs of human beings or indeed, the needs of nonhuman life forms with that we share this planet. But the Daoist and Confucian Ways taught opposite ways of living in harmonious balance with the ever-shifting expressions of *yin* and *yang* ceaselessly working in nature.

Both the Daoist and Confucian Ways originated as answers to the social and political anarchy of the Warring States Period (475–221 BCE). This was a time of political and social turbulence. The dominant issue of these dangerous times was how human beings could learn to live peacefully in community established on justice and compassion that mirrors the balancing flows of nature's processes. The classical Daoist Way asserted that all governmental systems are unnatural because they are artificial systems that force human beings to live in accordance with the collective egos of powerful political and economic elites imposing their standards on the majority of the community. It is governments that start wars, create poverty, and unjustly oppress human beings by forcing them to act unnaturally, meaning out of harmony with the Dao. So "compassion" and "justice" only occur when rulers govern by non-governing so that what is natural for human community can gradually evolve in harmony with the Dao.

The Confucian Way also based its distinctive teachings and practices on living in balanced harmony with the Dao, but in a way that sought to directly address the hard issues of statecraft. Daoist tradition was predominately a path of withdrawal from social engagement as its practitioners left settled communities to live solitary monastic lives mostly in isolated, small mountain communities. Confucian tradition was and remains a way of social engagement. Since both traditions originated during the end of the Period of the Warring States, both sought to answer a single question: How should human beings learn to live together in harmonious balance with the Dao? Each answered this question differently. But the Chinese people did not see the

Confucian Way and the Daoist Way as dual opposites that require choosing one and rejecting the other. Indeed if one thinks of the Daoist Way as a *yin* philosophy and the Confucian Way as a *yang* philosophy, the Chinese people sought to live in balanced harmony between them. There are times when one should primarily follow the Confucian Way, and there are times it is wise to follow the Daoist Way. So the Chinese Way of faith and practice is a wise balancing act between the Daoist Way and the Confucian Way. So what are the distinctive Confucian contributions to the Chinese Way?

From its beginnings, the Confucian Way has addressed the question of establishing just and compassionate community. Confucius (ca 550–480 BCE) and his most influential followers, including Mengzi (ca 370–290 BCE), attached great importance to proper, compassionately just relationships within families, communities, society, and the state. Historically, an emphasis on filial piety and reciprocity legitimated a patriarchal order in which the emperor was viewed as the father of his subjects, and the father as the master of his wife and family. Beginning with the Han Dynasty (206 BCE–220 CE) state-supported Confucian rites and sacrifices served to dramatize the harmony between Heaven, Earth, and humanity and underscored the ideally just compassion (yi) of the emperor's rule. In Confucian teaching, justice and compassion are not abstractions but rather concrete realizations of harmony and reciprocity in communal relationships working for the common God.

Specifically, early Confucian notions of justice and compassion appropriated the ancient idea of "the Mandate of Heaven," whereby successful rulers who presided over peace and prosperity were seen to possess divine favor. Unjust rulers who did not fulfill their obligations to society were liable to fall upon political and personal misfortune—evidence of the loss of Heaven's Mandate—that often led to rebellion against such a ruler so that Heaven's Mandate might be passed on to a new dynasty. Obviously, the Confucian Way is not the mystical Way of the Daoists, but a Way of social engagement with the political and ethical necessities for constructing human community.

◦ ◦ ◦

All of these examples from various faith traditions give evidence to a common spiritual thread woven throughout humanity, calling forth the best angels in all of us. In the last two chapters, we will explore the potential of finding a path toward mutual understanding in our quest for a more civil society.

Questions for Reflection

1. How is the "Golden Rule" an example of a common value among various religions traditions?

2. What are other common themes in various religions such as justice, mercy, and humility?

3. Do all the religions mentioned in this chapter view life as sacred?

4. What are some of the differences of emphasis that you noted in the various religious practices?

5. Why do you think that people of certain religious traditions are sometimes suspicious or fearful of those who believe or practice their faith differently?

6

Embracing Differences
The Gift of Religious Pluralism

> When the Messiah comes, there will be no more
> hate, beatings, or pain.
>
> **—Sholem Asch, from his play *The God of Vengeance***

A Christian, a Muslim, a Jew, and an atheist walk into a coffee shop. They talk, laugh, drink coffee, share stories, and become good friends. This is not intended to be a joke. This is what happens when people open their hearts and see the humanity in others.[1] This is exactly how it played out at one high school in Seattle, Washington. At the spring the commencement ceremony in June of 2019, two members of the graduating class of Nathan Hale High School paid tribute to how the administration and teachers had cultivated a culture of mutual respect and care among a very diverse student body. In a school district in which more than fifty different languages are spoken, educators were intentional about helping each student see themselves as a person of worth and potential. They created a safe environment in which young people of different ethnic and religious backgrounds could come together to learn from each other and support one another. Both students of color, the speakers agreed that their high school experience had enabled them to envision a better world and had encouraged them to use their young lives to make a difference for good in their communities.

Religious pluralism is not universalism. Rather it becomes an opportunity to view life and faith from a variety of perspectives. When Gene Roddenberry wrote the original *Star Trek* television series, he sought to embed each episode with an allegory and lesson in diversity. Roddenberry's scripts were intended to answer the questions posed by a pluralistic universe. *What does it mean to respect another culture, ethnic tradition, or religious practice? How do we make room for different points of view? How can we approach a given issue or problem from multiple perspectives?* These questions can serve us well today as we consider ways to build bridges among various ethnic groups and religious traditions.

Choosing Exodus or Exile

The Faith Action Network (FAN) is comprised of Christians of all sorts—Protestants representing most "mainline" denominations, Roman Catholics, Orthodox Christians, even a few "liberal" Evangelicals as well as Buddhists, Sunni, Shi'a, and Sufi Muslims, Sikhs, Native Americans representing the tribes of the Pacific Northwest, and those who identified themselves as "spiritual but not religious." The central purpose of FAN is creating opportunities for inter-religious dialogue between the various religious communities that populate Seattle and all cities and towns north to the Canadian border and west of the Cascade Mountains. These dialogues include: *conceptual dialogue* focused on the defining teachings of these religious Ways; *socially engaged dialogue*, focused on the distinctive views of these Ways on issues of social, economic, gender, and environmental justice; and *interior dialogue*, meaning active participation in the specific practices of each religious Way (i.e., meditation, contemplative prayer, or dancing with Dervishes). But, in fact, these three forms of dialogue are so interdependent that their separation is merely instrumental. What is most appealing about FAN is its collective refusal to engage in one form of dialogue over the other two. It is a wonderful interfaith community focused on achieving the common good for all human beings in interdependence with all sentient beings with whom we share life on Planet Earth.

The Keynote Speaker for a 2018 gathering of the organization was Rabbi Ruth Zlotnick, Senior Rabbi at Temple Beth Am in Seattle. The foundation of everything "Jewish," she noted, originated in the Exile of the People of Israel into slavery in Egypt and the Exodus led by Moses from slavery into the wilderness and eventually new life in "the Promised Land." The people had a choice, she said: "Either choose Exile or Exodus, either slavery or freedom, either fear or courage, either death or life." Searching for life is journeying to the Promised Land, a place of freedom and life that cannot be identified with any specific place on this planet, and "most certainly," she said, "with the State of Israel." The Promised Land is a place of shalom, a place of wholeness, compassionate justice, and community, a place of God's choosing and time. "It's not the arrival in the Promised Land that's important," she said. "It's by undertaking Exodus to the Promised Land that we can glimpse it here-and-now, but never fully, provided we choose Exodus." The Exodus journey is an ongoing journey.

Choosing Exodus means not clinging to the past. Choosing Exodus is incorporating the past into the present by learning from it without clinging to it through what Alfred N. Whitehead called "positive" and "negative apprehensions" as we envision future possibilities for individual and communal creative transformation. The Exodus journey requires rejecting any and all forms of racism and misogyny. Choosing Exodus means regarding the LGBT community as part of the human community; choosing Exodus means rejecting a free market capitalist economic system that seeks to strip the Earth bare of the natural resources necessary to support both human and nonhuman life on this planet. Choosing Exodus means replacing oil and coal with wind and solar power while training coal miners and petroleum workers for jobs in clean power industries. Choosing Exodus means breaking our addiction to gas-guzzling automobiles that make air unbreathable, as anyone who has driven a car on a Los Angeles freeway on a hot July day knows by experience and building energy efficient rapid transit systems capable of transporting large numbers of human beings efficiently and safely. Choosing Exodus means choosing nonviolence and refusing to cooperate with any and all governmental policies that require war. Choosing Exodus means resistance against any and all forms of discrimination based on gender, sexual orientation, race, or religion. Choosing Exodus means standing for justice and compassion as the heart of community building, as the Hebraic prophets and the historical Jesus instructed so long ago. The motivations for choosing Exodus and rejecting Exile are perhaps as numerous as the people undertaking an Exodus journey.

Countering Islamophobia

Muslims have been demonized worldwide since the September 11, 2001, attack on American soil by self-described Islamic terrorists or jihadists. While Islamic extremists make up only a small fraction of those throughout the world who adhere to the teachings of Mohammad, there were American politicians including presidential candidate Donald Trump who advocated for a national registry for all Muslims living in the United States as a way of identifying "threats to national security," a policy that is contrary to the Constitution. It's also not particularly "Christian," in spite of the opinion of some leaders from the Christian Right.

Christians in the local faith community of Pointe of Grace Lutheran Church in Mukilteo, Washington, along with other area congregations decided that if their Muslim brothers and sisters were ever required to declare their faith on a governmental registry, they would also add their names. After all, it makes perfect sense. "Islam" names the act of surrendering to God's will in all things, and "Muslim" names the one who surrenders to God's will as tested and measured by the Qur'an (the "Recitations) and the Sunna (stories about what Mohammed said and did). Christians also seek to surrender to God's will as reflected in the Lord's Prayer ("Your will be done") and the historical Jesus's struggle in the Garden of Gethsemane in prayer asking for God to "deliver" him from a death he knows he will suffer, yet willing to follow God's will, even if it meant death. In fact, the Muslims I know regard Jesus as "Muslim." To be sure, Muslims and Christians test and measure the meaning of "surrender" differently, but these differences pale into insignificance in actual dialogue with Muslims.

One of the best-known verses of the Qur'an declares, "Do you not know, O people, that I have made you into tribes and nations that you may know each other" (Surah 49:13). Of course, "to know each other" is an important goal of the practice of interreligious dialogue, particularly the dialogue with our Muslim brothers and sisters. "Knowing each other" requires breaching social, ethnic, gender, and religious boundaries. But our Muslim brothers and sisters often cite other Qur'anic advice regarding religious pluralism: "If God had so willed, he would have made you a single people, but his plan is to test you in what he has given you; so strive as a race in all virtues" (Surah 5:48).

Given the negative stereotypes about Islam that seem to be running amok in Europe and the United States often acted out by fire bombings of mosques and physical attacks against our Muslim brothers and sisters, it is necessary to counter Islamophobia with some factual information about Islam.

First, the literal meaning of the Arabic word *Islam* is "surrender." He or she who surrenders to God's will is a *Muslim*. But it's one thing to surrender to God's will, and it's quite another thing to understand how to surrender to God's will throughout the fourteen-hundred-year history of Islam. So Muslims test and measure this "how" by trying to conform to the Qur'an, whose words, Muslim's believe, are the actual instructions of God revealed to Mohammed through the Angel Gabriel, along with the Sunna or "custom" of the prophet Mohammed. The Sunna is a collection of stories about what Mohammed did or said about the specific demands of surrendering to God's will in actual living situations.

Second, both the Qur'an and the Sunna explicitly forbid terrorism, slavery, sex trafficking, the exploitation of women, and employing aggressive forms of violence for religious reasons like forced conversion to Islam or the persecution of non-Muslims—all of which are activities engaged in by extremist groups such as ISIS. Anyone engaging in violence for religious reasons, anyone engaging in terrorism, Muslim or non-Muslim, is not surrendering to God's will to live justly and compassionately in community.

In other words, "Islamic terrorism" is a fiction; groups like ISIS are simply terrorists. Likewise, there are no Christian or Jewish terrorist organizations. Groups like the Ku Klux Klan or individual persons claiming to be Christian who fire-bomb a mosque or Jews who terrorize Palestinians are neither Christian nor Jewish. They are simply terrorists. Faithful Muslims, Christians, or Jews are not terrorists.

Finally, monotheism is fundamental to Islamic, Christian, and Jewish teachings and practices. All three religious Ways stress surrendering to God's will that human beings live justly and compassionately in community with one another and with the sentient beings that share life with human beings on Planet Earth. Of course, the meaning of "surrendering to God's will" is tweaked differently. Muslims test and measure the meaning of surrender by the Qur'an, our Jewish brothers and sisters by the Torah—the first five books of the Hebrew scriptures—and Christians by the New Testament, particularly by the four gospels and the epistles of Saint Paul. Of course, there are differences. But the differences pale to insignificance in comparison to what all three religious Ways share in common.

For these reasons, no non-Muslim needs to fear our Muslim brothers and sisters. Human beings are one in our diversity, including our religious diversity, as the Jewish Way, the Christian Way, and the Islamic Way affirm in their own distinctive teachings and practices. The most faithful way to surrender to God's will is the practice of interreligious dialogue so that we may know each other and hereby learn from each other. Life is too short to live in fear of our Muslim neighbors. Rather we can embrace them as faith-filled sisters and brothers.

The Universal Nature of Faith

On a Sunday morning in about 2010, when a fall day's new sunlight seemed to catch in the trees like fog and hang over the land, changing colors but never fading, a pastor preached a sermon about the universal nature of faith. The preacher noted how from mud huts in Africa to great cathedrals in Europe, Christians were kneeling to receive the elements of the Eucharist. She drew an impressive picture of the diversity or, more accurately, the "pluralism" of Christian faith. An example of this is illustrated by the hymn "In Christ There Is No East or West," sung by many Christian denominations: "Join hands, disciples of the faith, whate'er your race may be. All children of the living God are surely kin to me."[2]

Someone engaged in Christian worship might wonder what other faithful persons were doing at that moment. One might consider a Muslim, bowing on all fours at a mosque at Al Azar University in Cairo in surrender to the will of God which defines the practice of Islam. In Japan, a Buddhist meditation teacher is anchored in an evening session of *zazen* or "seated meditation," seeking to follow the Path of the Buddha in a seven-hundred-year-old monastery. In Seattle, an eighty-five-year-old Shingon Buddhist nun, her body made tired by her years, is spending the morning chanting a healing mantra on behalf of an old friend whose life is running out because she believes the Buddha's compassion extends to persons in various states of being—those in the process of dying as well as those mourning for a dying teacher and friend. In Calcutta a physician-monk of the Ramakrishna Order is offering his skills to help the suffering and dying the way most Hindus offer flowers to an image of God because he sees his patients as *avatars*—"incarnations" of Brahman. In Wisconsin, a convert to Tibetan Buddhism had completed a complicated morning ritual in front of the mandala she established as her home alter, while a Trappist monk in Massachusetts was spending his day in a silent interior pilgrimage of his own.

In his ground-breaking book *The Universal Christ*, Richard Rohr makes the radical suggestion that God can hold together people of faith from a diversity of religious backgrounds. He believes that we are on the cusp of a two-thousand-year-old paradigm shift from Judaism and Christianity to an embrace of the Universal Christ. Suggesting that this was too monumental an idea for the first two thousand years of Christianity, Rohr writes:

> Every religion, each in its own way, is looking for the gateway, the conduit, the Sacrament, the Avatar, the finger that points to the moon. We need someone to model and exemplify the journey from physical incarnation, through a rather ordinary human existence, through trials and death, and into a Universal Presence unlimited by space and time (which we call "resurrection"). Most of us know about Jesus walking this journey, but far fewer know that Christ is the collective and eternal manifestation of the same—and that "the Christ" image includes all of us and everything. [Saint] Paul was overwhelmed by this recognition, and it became the core of his entire message . . . Jesus can hold together one group or religion. Christ can hold together everything.
>
> In fact, Christ already does this; it is we who resist such wholeness, as if we enjoy our arguments and our divisions into parts. Yet throughout the Scriptures, we were given statements like these: "When everything is reconciled in him . . . God will be all in all." (*1 Corinthians 15:28*). . . . "All fullness is found in him, through him all things are reconciled, everything in heaven and everything on earth." (*Colossians 1:19–20*)

This is not heresy, universalism, or a cheap version of Unitarianism. This is the Cosmic Christ, who always was, who became incarnate in time, and who is still being revealed.[3]

A History of Religious Pluralism

Religious pluralism is a fact of human existence. It is a theological interpretation of the empirical facts of religious diversity. Because of geographical distances, ancient and pre-modern human communities could be culturally isolated, although never totally. Which means that encountering the "religious other" was a different experience for them than it was for sixteenth century Christians and is different again for twenty-first century Christians. For example, the only non-Christians that Europeans would have encountered were Jews as caricatured through the anti-Judaism of the New Testament and the anti-Semitism ingredient in Late Medieval theology and the early European Renaissance. The only Muslims they knew anything about were referred to as "the Turks," who were a dangerous military threat on the borders of Eastern Europe. Like everyone else in sixteenth century Europe, one's knowledge of Islam was filtered through secondhand stereotypes originating in the violence of the Crusades.

But pluralism was still a fact of life and a theological concern within the Late Medieval Catholic Church and the churches of the Reformation. Both Lutheran and Reformed theologians confronted this pluralism as a challenge, the focus of which was hammering out communal identity mostly in relation to "the other." That is to say, Martin Luther and other "evangelical" reformers sought to define a distinctively "Lutheran" communal identity over against Reformed communities and the Roman Catholic Church. Reformed and Catholic theologians were engaged in the same enterprise. Here, religious pluralism was encountered not so much as positive, but as a threat to church unity and proper Christian identity.

Luther and the other Reformers lived in a time when non-orthodoxy and "heresy" could cost a person his or her life and they were often the source of bloody wars. One had to be careful in defining one's religious identity to make sure it sounded "Christian" to orthodox authorities. Luther, after all, took great pains to make clear that he was not trying to start a new church. In his view, he was calling the Catholic Church back to a Pauline tradition filtered through the theology of Saint Augustine that he believed had been repressed by the Catholicism of his day.

At this point, it would be good to summarize the meaning of "religious pluralism" as distinguished from "religious diversity":

- **Pluralism is not just another name for "diversity."** Pluralism goes beyond merely naming the empirical fact of the existence of different religious Ways among human being. Pluralism is active theological engagement with the diversity of religious Ways. We can study diversity, celebrate it, and complain about it, as Reformation theologians often did, and contemporary theologians often do, but diversity alone is not pluralism.

- **Pluralism is an attitude, a theological orientation, a theoretical construct.** Given the strong exclusivism of traditional Christian claims about the historical Jesus as the Christ of faith, a theology of religions, of which pluralism is one option, is a strictly Christian enterprise. Non-Christians do not normally encounter religious diversity or pluralism as problematic in the same way as Christians.

- **Pluralism as a theoretical construct is neither an ideology nor a Western-neo-liberal scheme.** Pluralism is best understood as a dynamic process through which we dialogically engage with religious Ways other than our own through our deepest differences. Pluralism is not mere tolerance of "the other," but an active attempt to understand "the other." Pluralism is a theological-philosophical move beyond mere tolerance toward understanding of what to make of the empirical facts of religious diversity.

- **Pluralism is not debilitating relativism.** It does not eliminate deep religious or secular commitments. Many critics of pluralism persist in linking pluralism to a kind of valueless relativism, in which all perspectives are equally compelling and, as a result, equally not compelling. Pluralism, they contend, undermines commitment to one's own religious Way by watering down particularity in the interest of universality. Such views are a distortion because pluralism is engagement with, not abandonment of, differences. While encountering people of other religious Ways may lead to less myopic views of one's own Way, pluralism is not based on reductive relativism.

- **The language of pluralism is dialogue—Vigorous engagement and argument are essential to a democratic society and to Christian community.** Dialogue is vital so that we appropriate our faith not by habit or heritage alone, but by making it our own within the context of conversations with people of other religious Ways. Dialogue is not aimed at achieving mere agreement but achieving relationship. Dialogue as the language of pluralism is the language of engagement, involvement, and participation.

- **As a theological construct, pluralism is never a completed project but the ongoing work of each generation.**

The Challenge and the Promise of Incarnational Theology

Christian experience of God as incarnated in the historical Jesus as the Christ of faith is the main push toward a pluralistic theology of religions. The doctrine of the Incarnation is what structures the experience of all faithful Christians because all distinctively Christian teachings and practices are interpretations of the meaning and implications of the Incarnation. Since there exist a substantial number of interpretations of the Incarnation, Christian faith and practices exhibits locally the pluralism that exists universally in all of the world's religious Ways. Historically, the meaning of the Doctrine of the Incarnation has been the heart of Christian theological exclusivism, meaning that faith in the Incarnation is the key to God's salvific action in the world and therefore non-Christian Ways are superseded by the Christian Way.

But it is also possible, as noted by Richard Rohr's suggestion, that the Incarnation can be interpreted as a push toward more pluralistic openness towards the world's religious Ways as well as the diversity ingredient within the Christian Way itself. This "push" comes from Christian experience of God as mysterious and Trinitarian. There is also a third push: historical consciousness that suggests all knowledge is relative.[4] Human knowledge of anything, including knowledge of God, is limited by the cultural and historical points of view we occupy at the moment we claim to know anything. If this is true, historical consciousness teaches us that the reality of God, whom Christians apprehend incarnated in the historical Jesus as the Christ of faith, is not limited by what Christians apprehend. Accordingly, while historical consciousness tells us that any glimpse of truth we can have is intrinsically finite, "religious experience" contextualized by the historicity of all knowledge tells us that God is more than any human being or community can apprehend. This means Christian experience has a paradoxical edge: any particular encounter with God is as mysterious as it is real, as ambiguous as it is reliable. Mystics and non-mystic theologians who have sensed this recognition populate the history of the Christian Way: St. Paul, Athanasius, Symon the New Theologian, Gregory Palamas, Augustine, Irenaeus, Thomas Aquinas, Julian or Norwich, Meister Eckhart, Marguerite Porete, Martin Luther, John

Calvin, and most recently, Karl Rahner, Edward Schillebeekx, Thomas Merton, Paul Tillich, Daniel Day Williams, Paul Knitter, and John B. Cobb, Jr.

Affirming that we cannot know everything about God does not mean that we cannot know something. In agreement with Martin Luther, *The Augsburg Confession* affirms that while "knowledge of God" is possible for all human beings rationally deduced from the laws of nature (i.e., "natural theology"), true knowledge of God comes to Christians through faith, meaning "trust" in God's act of salvation through the historical Jesus as the Christ. In other words, true knowledge of God comes to Christians at the moment of faith rather than our own merits.[5] So the heart of Christian faith and practice is the Incarnation: in the life, death, and resurrection of a particular human being two thousand years ago in a backwater region of the Roman Empire, humanity encountered God within the reality of historical existence. No question. Or in the words of Luther's *Small Catechism*, "This is most certainly true."

But while the historical Jesus reveals God, the Incarnation does not reveal all that God is. Most Christians talk about the Incarnation as "God in human form" or the "fullness of the divine mystery" in the historical Jesus or the Christian Right's unqualified assertion that "Jesus is God" which violates the meaning of the Incarnation more than preserving it. Affirming the Incarnation does not mean that the historical Jesus took on *all* that constitutes God, or that God took on *all* that constitutes being human. So, while the historical Jesus, as the second *persona* of the Trinity, defines *who* God is for Christians, the historical Jesus does not exhaust *what* God is. To ignore the limitations of the Incarnation is to fall into Docetism—the heresy that stresses the divinity of Jesus as it denatures his humanity. Much mainline, popular, and fundamentalist Christian exclusivist theology is docetic.

Grace as a Religious Principal

So, here's the question: "If there is only one God, why are there so many different religions?" Anyone who studies the religious Ways of humanity will witness great creativity and great stupidity among representatives of all the religious Ways. Still, it's the creative persons who stand out—faithful Christians, Buddhists, Jews, Muslims, Hindus, and Native Americans—living integrated lives within the rough-and-tumble of historical existence. They remind us that no single religious Way can make claims to be the final repository of truth. This fact constitutes the main empirical evidence that falsifies the theological imperialism of universal truth claims, both Christian and non-Christian.

Consequently, when it comes down to it, *we are justified by grace through faith* as suggested by Martin Luther's interpretation of the New Testament message according to Saint Paul. The experience of grace and faith are not absent from any of the world's religious Ways, even though each religious Way has its own core teachings and practices that are different from the Christian Way.

Justification by grace through faith never occurs in a vacuum. Chances are persons born in a Muslim culture, would be Muslims. Had they been born in China or Japan, chances are they would be Buddhist or Confucian Daoist or Shintoist, or perhaps Muslim if our parents were from Central Asia. Born in Palestine, persons might be Jewish, Muslim, Christian, or none of the above. Even so, in the end, one's particular faith is a matter of being "struck from one's horse."* When, or if, this happens, the religious Way one inherits is shown to have a depth of which one was not previously aware. One hears not only the lyrics of a Religious Way but also its music. It ultimately depends on "who" or "what" speaks to us. One can admire Mahatma Gandhi, Mohammed, the Buddha and the Jewish sages. The Sufi poets and the Hindu epics can make one's heart sing. The socially engaged Buddhist faith of Sulik Sivaraksa and the Dalai Lama may challenge and inspire others.

God's character as compassionate wisdom and justice is modeled for Christians by the historical Jesus as the Christ of faith. Christians are called to unconditionally love all human beings and other creatures of God's creation wisely, as God loves all human beings and other creatures of God's creation wisely, with no strings attached. Such love is not detached but passionately involved. We are interdependent, meaning we are brothers and sisters because the existence of creation originates with God. We should therefore relate to one another according to what is needed and necessary, which may often be different from what is wanted. In this sense, love is non-personal: like rain falling on the Earth, God's loving compassion falls on all without regard to social status, economic influence, merit, or religious tradition, so don't take it personally. But the interdependent flip-side of unconditional love is justice, which the prophetic tradition from which Jesus lived and taught is liberation from all institutional and personal obstacles that cause suffering and prevent human beings from achieving what they need for meaningful life in community with one another, with nature, and with God. Love as the nonviolent struggle for justice for all human beings as well as for other sentient beings is involved and passionate.

In other words, for Christians, love of God—the First Commandment—engenders the Second Commandment: unbounded love guided by compassionate wisdom that takes priority over all other ethical injunctions, religious

---

*Refers to the conversion of St. Paul when he encountered a vision of Christ and fell off his horse.

practices, theological formulations, and institutional demands. The Second Commandment means that loving one's neighbor has priority over proclaiming doctrine or formally worshipping God. The New Testament's instruction is this: first work out things with your neighbor, brother, or sister, then go to church or synagogue or mosque or temple (Matthew 5:23–24). Don't allow religious practices, with its professions of creeds and liturgical observances get in the way of doing good for your neighbor. It's better to break the Sabbath than to fail in loving our neighbors. (Matthew 12:12)

Viewed from the role loving compassionate wisdom played in the faith and practice of Jesus, there is something fundamentally wrong with traditional views of other religious Ways. For a starter, to practice loving compassionate wisdom means engaging non-Christians in dialogue, not as "other," but as persons who in mutual interdependence with us seek truth. Dialogue means treating them as we would want them to treat us. It means listening to their witness to truth as we would want them to listen to ours. It means confronting them when we think they are wrong, even as we must be willing to be confronted by them when they think we are wrong. In short, to love one's neighbor justly and compassionately means to be in dialogue with them.

Moving Beyond Exclusivity and Inclusivity to Authentic Dialogue

Here's the rub. Traditional Christian attitudes toward the world's religious Ways—both exclusive and inclusive theologies of religions—can be obstacles to treating our religious neighbors with love in dialogue. An exclusive theology interprets all religious Ways different from our own as false. Persons participating in these "other" Ways are in error and in need of conversion to one's own religious Way. An inclusive theology asserts that whatever truth exists in a religious Way other than our own is a partial, incomplete reflection of the full truth of one's own religious Way. Thus, persons participating in these traditions are not in complete error but they still need conversion to the full truth of one's particular religious Way in order to be in full contact with saving truth. Both models are in conflict with the practice of loving compassionate dialogue.

For Christians the questions are these: (1) Can we respect our non-Christian brother and sisters and be open to them if we must assert before we even meet them that our truth is better than theirs, that they are inferior to us in what they hold to be true and sacred? And (2) Can we affirm and love them when we are convinced with a priori certainty that they will have to agree with our truth in order to arrive at the fullness of God's truth? Whenever we hold up any truth claim and insist that according to the will of God it is the only or the absolutely final norm according to which other truths must be measured, we are unable to treat non-Christians as our sisters and brothers. While absolutizing the Christian Way into a universal norm for measuring all non-Christian Ways *does* enable us to *confront* non-Christians as "other," it *does not* allow us to *encounter* them or *be encountered* by them as sisters and brothers, as loving compassionate wisdom requires.

Essentially, the conflict many Christians experience is between theological orthodoxy—right beliefs—and orthopraxy—right behavior. Partly this has to do with the fact that as more Christians come to personally know non-Christians, it has become clear that our non-Christian sisters and brothers in general are neither less nor more kind, thoughtful, loving, compassionate, or just than Christians. Increasingly, Christians are experiencing tension, if not contradiction, between the first and second commandments—to spread the Gospel to all nations as they extend love to all human beings and creatures of the Earth guided by compassionate wisdom. While the historical Jesus instructed his disciples to love their neighbors as themselves, he is also said to have given them a "third commandment"—to go forth into the world and make his message known to all human beings. Christians are called upon to love their neighbors as themselves and to make the good news about Jesus known to all human beings so as to make disciples of all human beings.

Yet for whatever reason Christians have tended to make this "third commandment" more important than the First and Second commandment, or at least the criterion for practicing the First and Second commandments, throughout Christian history. Christians have spread the Gospel throughout the world but they have all too often not loved non-Christians justly, wisely, or compassionately in the process. The result is that Christians share a long history of not listening to, learning from, or affirming non-Christians as loving compassionate wisdom requires.

The theological and ethical contradictions between the first and second commandments and the last command of Jesus, between Christian ethical practice and Christian doctrine, between orthopraxy and orthodoxy has a long history. However, given the priority of the orthopraxy of loving one's neighbor as oneself wisely and compassionately—as illustrated by Mark's account of the historical Jesus and the epistles of Saint Paul—exclusive and inclusive models for understanding our final commission should be rejected and replaced by the practice of interreligious dialogue guided by loving compassionate wisdom. It's not that theological reflection is unimportant. Theology is, after all, faith-seeking understanding. But doctrinal orthodox is not more important than the practice of unbounded love and compassionate wisdom. Like everything else in the universe, the practice of loving compassionate wisdom and theological reflection are interdependent.

We conclude that it is possible to enter into authentic dialogue with those of other faith traditions while holding to the truth of one's own beliefs; and at the same time respecting the faith practices of our neighbors. What is important is that we recognize that we have much to learn from each other. We can be open to inviting God's Spirit to intercede and bless us with compassion and understanding for each other as we will see in the following chapter.

Questions for Reflection

1. How do you understand the difference between choosing exile and exodus?

2. What are some teachings from the Islamic tradition that you find helpful or interesting?

3. What is your reaction to Richard Rohr's description of the Cosmic Christ? How does he contribute to the conversation about religious pluralism?

4. How might you and your faith community engage with persons of another religious tradition?

5. What are some of the obstacles to authentic inter-religious dialogue?

Building Bridges of Hope
Ten Ways Forward

When the power of love overcomes the love of
power, we will know peace.

—Jimmy Hendrix

The turbulent 1960s in America saw a number of political and religious heroes cut down in their prime for standing up for what they believed. Among them were the Rev. Dr. Martin Luther King Jr., President John F. Kennedy, and Senator Robert Kennedy. When serving as attorney general, Robert Kennedy persuaded his brother John to deal with the racial divide in the country. They were compelled by the tenets of their Roman Catholic faith to act on behalf of the oppressed and disadvantaged. Choosing to take a political risk on this controversial subject, President Kennedy addressed the nation from the Oval Office with these words:

This nation was founded by men of many nations and backgrounds. It was founded on the principle that all men are created equal and that the rights of every man are diminished when the rights of one man are threatened. Today we are committed to worldwide struggle to promote and protect the rights of all who wish to be free. It ought to be possible for every American to enjoy the privileges of being American without regard to his race, or color. In short, every American ought to have the right to be treated as he or she would wish to be treated.[1]

Five months later, President Kennedy was assassinated. Taking up his brother's mantle, Robert Kennedy then ran for the Democratic nomination for president in 1968. Seeking to be a "bridge builder" like his brother, he ran on a platform of inclusion, fairness, and justice for all Americans. On the night of his victory in the California primary, he too was gunned down. His vision for the nation—as with the Reverend King who was killed just two months before him—was for a positive and hopeful future in which all people regardless of race, creed, or economic status would flourish.

There have been other visionaries before and since, many of them whose lives were cut short because it seems the world cannot abide those who both condemn evil and envision a brighter future. It appears from the current climate of division, hatred, and violence that we still have a long way to go. Yet people of faith and those of no faith can make a difference if we but take up the mantle of being *bridge builders* and work together for the common good. This chapter suggests ten ways that we can move forward from our present state of division and despair and ensure a better tomorrow for our children and grandchildren around the globe.

WAY ONE:
Recognize and Repent of One's Offenses

There are many ways that individuals and groups have of causing others injury and pain. Examples have been cited throughout this book. In an effort to help the reader become more self-aware, here are seven ways that we can offend another:

1. *We demonize the other.* This is to regard another person—especially the stranger—as evil. We suggest they may be emotionally unstable, physically violent or dangerous, and of malicious intent.
2. *We trivialize the other.* We make light of a situation or dismiss the other person's concern as not all that important. When we joke about the stereotype of race, culture, or religion, we belittle others. Our aim is to make them feel small.
3. *We standardize the other.* We presume that we are all really the same and that any differences would be eliminated if we knew each other better. While the comment "We are all children of God" may be well intended, it can trivialize the unique differences of another person's culture or religion.
4. *We colonize the other.* We want to transform the other so that they will take on our perspective and adopt our way of thinking and believing. We want them to be like us. This means we often treat them as inferior to us or as not living up to our standards.

5. *We discount the other.* We ignore another person's idea or contribution or even overlook their presence. Often because we fear what they have to say or what they represent, we choose to make them invisible or deny their importance.
6. *We generalize the other.* When we categorize someone as representing a group or particular ideology, we don't have to deal with them as an individual. It becomes easier to dismiss people and overlook their uniqueness.
7. *We romanticize the other.* When we hold someone in unusually high esteem because of their fame or position of power, it is difficult to recognize them as fully human. We may think of a person as superior or more special than ourselves. We may choose to overlook their faults and mistakes because we idolize them. This makes it difficult to really know someone as they actually are and to establish an honest relationship.[2]

WAY TWO:
Stand in Solidarity with the Oppressed

Whatever our faith tradition, we are called to stand in solidarity with the oppressed and those on the margins. In the constitution of the Evangelical Lutheran Church in America one reads: "Every ordained minister shall speak publicly to the world in solidarity with the poor and oppressed, calling for justice and proclaiming God's love for the world."[3] In other documents, church members are exhorted to do the same as a way of living out their baptismal covenant with God and one another.

We find an example of this in Sweden. Attacks on Jews have doubled in the US from 2017 to 2018 and continued to increase; with the *New York Times* observing in an April 2019 editorial that violence against Jews had surged from the Internet and onto the streets. Likewise, anti-Semitism is flourishing worldwide. Many Jews in Europe feel under assault. The Nordic Resistance movement in Sweden has a toxic goal: to rid Sweden of all Jews. Amid the threats and violence, many Jews have chosen to forgo affixing the traditional miniature prayer scrolls called *mezuzahs* to their doorposts, and men may choose not to wear skullcaps outside of worship in public. However, there are signs of hope.

A Hasidic rabbi in Malmo, Sweden, organized a protest march that was intended to be a demonstration of faith, in order to stand up to the haters. He invited both Jewish and non-Jewish citizens to wear the traditional skullcaps called *kippahs* in protest against anti-Semitism. After Sabbath prayers, the rabbi requested that congregants not remove their kippahs as they left to go out into the streets. Fearful, some said, "They will kill us!" However, the walk proceeded in a peaceful manner, and they were joined by others not of the Jewish faith who wore skullcaps in solidarity. Now there are regular "kippah" walks in Malmo, Stockholm, and Berlin. Their fellow citizens in those places are standing with their Jewish sisters and brothers in a show of unity and mutual respect.[4]

Not long ago Temple Beth El Synagogue in Fargo, North Dakota, reached out to St. Mark's Lutheran Church when the congregation needed a worship space. The Jewish community invited their Christian sisters and brothers to share their sanctuary. They hope their collaboration will send a message of tolerance and inclusion to their community.

WAY THREE:
Educate and Work for Peace

"Blessed are the peacemakers for they will be called children of God," proclaimed Jesus in his Sermon on the Mount (Matthew 5:9). For some, peacemaking has been a high calling. It is the effort to resolve conflict and promote understanding among members of the human race. We recall the efforts of leaders like Dag Hammarskjöld, late Secretary General of the United Nations as well as presidents Carter and Reagan. In fact, the United Nations was founded in part to take the lead in resolving conflict and promoting peace among nations.

Closer to home is Seattle's **Peace Camp,** which every summer brings together Muslim, Jewish, and Christian children in an effort to forge bonds across these disparate communities. A fifteen-year-old Muslim girl named Mahmoud, admitted, "Camp made me break stereotypes that I would've had before if I didn't have any Christian or Arab friends. It's made me more of a peacemaker." She went on to say, "Yes, Jews, Muslims, and Christians do actually get along. We forget that all the same things are happening to each community." And then she added, "You don't have hate when you're born. You learn it. That's why this camp is so important." A youth leader named Oron, who is Israeli, believes that the camp helps participants realize that they are all children of God and states: "It's really important for me that we talk to our families and our communities and start changing the way we think. We're divided because people fail to see each other's humanity. We are more alike than we are different."[5]

WAY FOUR:
Assess Your Degree of Prejudice or Openness to Others

Racism has been defined as the systemic oppression of one group of people, sanctioned by a country, majority, or ruling class. Racism is a kind of prejudice that comes with power—where one group sees themselves as superior to another. Racism can be likened to an iceberg. We see only what's above the surface, but lurking underneath may be a whole pattern—often unknown or unrecognized—of prejudice, bigotry, hatred, fear of the other, discomfort over difference, or preconceived notions of another's race or culture, and the list goes on.

Those who deny they are racist would do well to look into their own heart and soul. For if the truth be known, every one of us possesses a prejudice of some kind when it comes to people who are different from us. We can identify five types of racism as follows: (1) **blatant** racism of which we are aware and is obvious to others; (2) **covert** racism of which we are aware but seek to keep hidden from others; (3) **unintentional** racism that we are unaware of, such as the telling of jokes about another's culture and not realizing they may not be funny; (4) a **self-righteousness** that claims we are not racist when we are in denial of our racist attitudes; and (5) **internalized** racism which is often the symptom of systemic racism. The latter can be found among certain groups where there is inbred prejudice or hatred toward a particular ethnic or religious group.[6]

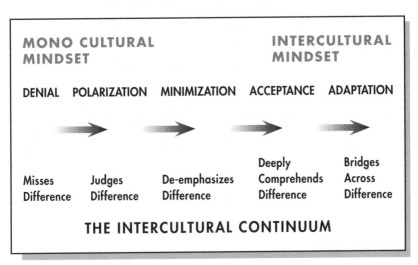

MONO CULTURAL MINDSET			INTERCULTURAL MINDSET	
DENIAL	POLARIZATION	MINIMIZATION	ACCEPTANCE	ADAPTATION
Misses Difference	Judges Difference	De-emphasizes Difference	Deeply Comprehends Difference	Bridges Across Difference

THE INTERCULTURAL CONTINUUM

The **Intercultural Continuum** is a way to assess one's tendency to discriminate or judge those who are different and shows the progression from a *Mono Cultural Mindset* to an *Intercultural Mindset.* The first stage is that of DENIAL in which one misses the differences. The second stage is POLARIZATION in which one judges the difference. The third stage is MINIMALIZATION in which one de-emphasizes the difference. The next state is ACCEPTANCE in which one deeply comprehends the difference. The last stage is ADAPTATION in which one is actually able to bridge across differences. In her book, *Developing Cultural Sensitivity and Competence*, Helen Fagan builds on the work of Milton Bennett in showing how one can bridge behavior across cultural differences.[7] Fagan is best known for her work in the area of diversity and cultural sensitivity. For example, in her work with medical students she used the Intercultural Development ment Inventory (IDI) to help them understand that their level of cultural competence impacts how they approach their patient's cultural differences. The IDI uses the Intercultural Continuum to illustrate how one might progress in one's understanding and appreciation for those different from oneself. Fagan administered the IDI at the beginning and end of her courses and the results showed growth in her students' level of cultural competence.

WAY FIVE:
Engage in Storytelling with
Those Different from Yourself

One of the things that helps build relationships and bind people to one another is storytelling; this is the sharing of personal stories about life, family, and culture. People are hungry for stories told in community with one another—whether it be an opportunity to share one's own story or listen to another's life journey. It can help build connection and bridge differences between people, especially in a multicultural setting. There is a something powerful about knowing others may have had a similar experience or faced some of the same challenges. Finally, it can build relationships and a sense of community where none existed before.

Faith communities can give people a voice to share their stories by providing a safe place and setting guidelines for sharing and truth-telling such as the following:

R   Take RESPONSIBILITY for what we say
    and feel without blaming others.

E   Practice
    EMPATHETIC listening.

S   Be SENSITIVE to differences in communication
    styles and feelings of others.

P   PONDER
    what we hear and feel before we speak.

E   EXAMINE
    our own assumptions and perceptions.

C   Keep CONFIDENTIALITY
    for the sake of healthy community.

T   TOLERATE
    aright or wrong. We can agree to disagree.[8]

Stories carry meaning and communicate values. They can be healing. Sometimes stories do some heavy lifting as in the sharing of a testimony or witness, whether it be about one's faith life or what someone learned from a life experience such as a battle with cancer or alcoholism.

Genuine storytelling requires that people be honest and forthright in the telling of their story. There is no right or wrong way to tell one's story, though one is encouraged to be as open and intimate as one feel comfortable. Sometimes it is helpful to start the sharing of stories by giving people questions to reflect on such as (a) "When was your happiest or most joyful moment in the past year?" or (b) "What do you wish more people knew about you or your life's experience?"

Listening is the key to good storytelling. The hearer is encouraged to withhold judgment as they listen to another share his or her story. It is helpful to put oneself in the other's place, to imagine what it must have been like to have a particular experience. Identify with the storyteller as much as possible. Consider what meaning or theme underlies the story. The following questions can help the listener reflect on the impact of the story: (a) "Is there a greater truth the teller is trying to communicate?" (b) "What lessons has one learned from the story? (c) "How is that person's story different or how is it the same as mine?" and (d) "How has the story helped to bridge any differences between the teller and the hearer?"

WAY SIX:
Participate in Interfaith Conversation

Dialogue among people of different faith traditions can be both challenging and rewarding. Many religious organizations such as the World Council of Churches or various denominations have been engaged in dialogue with other Christian groups for decades. In recent years this has been expanded to include non-Christian faith-based groups in an effort to promote mutual respect and a better understanding of one another's traditions; and in some cases to explore the potential of partnering together to address some of society's ills and especially to counter xenophobia or intolerance of another's religion.

There are a number of inter-faith organizations such as Neighbors in Faith that are hosting seminars in churches, synagogues, mosques, and community centers where people of various faith traditions can gather to learn about each other's religious beliefs and cultures. Some Christian congregations will invite both an imam and a rabbi to come and share their faith practices. In Duluth, Minnesota, Christians and Muslims gather for "Dinner and Dialogue" in area churches and mosques. A professor at the local community college who is a Muslim from Somali initiated the program a couple of years ago and reports that it has resulted in a better understanding of one another and helped participants see their commonality, such as both having Abrahamic origins. *Table Fellowship* has been practiced throughout the centuries, and significant relationships have often been made over a meal. Most importantly, these meals have helped bridge differences, and it has led to the building of new friendships among people of different faith traditions.

Some Inter-Religious Ground Rules:

1. The purpose is to learn, change, and grow, and to act on those new understandings.
2. Such dialogue must be two-sided, within each community and between communities.
3. Each person must be honest and sincere and assume the same from the dialogue partners.

4. Members must define themselves and be able to recognize themselves in the other group's expressed portrayal of their tradition.
5. People should come to the dialogue without strong assumptions about points of disagreement.
6. Dialogue should happen between equals, for example, not between Christian clergy and Hindu lay people.
7. Participants must be willing to look critically at themselves and their own traditions.
8. Each member should try to experience the other's religion "from within."[9]

WAY SEVEN:
Get to Know Your Community

How well do we know our communities? Those of us who live in a part of the country where there is a diverse population have an opportunity to interact with a variety of people. Where the population is more homogenous, it may be more difficult to find those who are different from us in religion, race, or culture. However, we must start where we are and begin our journey of discovery. We may be surprised at the hidden gems we will find as we become better acquainted with the members of our community.

The first step is to learn about the context of our neighborhood and larger community. We can go online or check with our local city hall to discover the ethnic, religious, and economic make-up of our neighbors. Even those who have lived for some time in a community may not be aware of the changing demographics of their area, so it is good to do some research.

A second step is to reach out to community leaders and find out what they perceive to be the needs, concerns, and challenges facing your neighbors. Make an appointment to meet with your local city council representative, the principal of one of the neighborhood schools, the director of the area senior center or YMCA, and/or a religious leader. Most will welcome a conversation with a concerned citizen who wants to know more about their community. Prepare some interview questions that might include the following: (1) "How long have you been serving in this community?" (2) "What have you found most rewarding about living and working here?" (3) "What do you think are some of the greatest needs or challenges facing our community?" (4) "What are your thoughts about how we might better address those concerns together?"

Another step is crucial if there are recent immigrants who live in the community. And that is to be aware of the process of *acculturation*. This has to do with how an individual or family group handles the transition to a new culture. There can be one of four outcomes: *assimilation*, in which the immigrant accepts the new culture and rejects their culture of origin; *marginalization*, in which the individual rejects both their culture of origin and the new culture; *separation*, in which the person or group keeps the culture of origin and chooses to reject their new culture; and *integration*, in which the person new to this country is able to both maintain the dignity and beauty of their own culture while at the same time embracing a new culture. It is important to note that each person or family new to the community—whether from another nation or another part of the country—will face a time of adjustment.

Finally, act on what has been learned. There may be some new relationships—even friendships—that have been developed and can now be nurtured. You may find you have some gifts or talents that are needed in service to the larger community. Hopefully, you will have a better understanding and informed perspective about the people with whom you live.

WAY EIGHT:
Embrace Diversity and Reject Nationalism

We live in a global community where what affects one nation or people affects all. Nationalism stands as perhaps the greatest threat facing our nation and our world today, for it assumes—especially in the case of the United States—that we are somehow superior to the rest of the world or that we can selfishly focus on ourselves and our own needs without regard to the plight of the rest of human life on this planet. On the season five premier of the CBS television series, *Madam Secretary*, the lead character, Secretary of State Elizabeth McCord, delivers a stirring speech:

> I am convinced that nationalism is the existential threat of our time. Now I want to be clear. Nationalism is not the same as patriotism. It's a perversion of patriotism. Nationalism, the belief system held by those who attacked us, promotes the idea that inclusion and diversity represent weakness, that the only way to succeed is to give blind allegiance to the supremacy of one race over all others. Nothing could be less American. Patriotism, on the other hand, is about building each other up and embracing our diversity as the source of our nation's strength. 'We the people' means *all* the people. America's heroes didn't die for race or region. They died for the ideals enshrined in our Constitution. Above all, free-

dom from tyranny, which requires our unwavering support of a free press; freedom of religion, all religions; the right to vote, and making sure nothing infringes on any of those rights, which belong to us all. Look where isolationism has gotten us in the past. Two world wars. Seventy million dead. Never again can we go back to those dark times when fear and hatred, like a contagion, infected the world. That, as much as ending the threat of nuclear war, is what today is about.

And it is why we must never lose sight of our common humanity, our common values, and our common decency. I was reminded recently of our nation's founding motto, *E pluribus unum*. Out of many, one. Thirteen disparate colonies became one country. One people. And today, we call on all Americans and people everywhere to reject the scourge of nationalism. Because governments can't legislate tolerance or eradicate hate. That's why each one of us has to find the beauty in our differences instead of the fear. Listen instead of reacting. Reach out instead of recoiling. It's up to us. All of us. Thank you.[10]

Christian nationalism is an even greater danger that seeks to merge Christian and American identities that end up distorting both the Christian faith and American's constitutional democracy. The union of the two is seen as a threat both to faith communities and our democracy. For a union of the two would lead to a theocracy in which religious freedom would be surrendered to those in power. A group called "Christians Against Christian Nationalism" have drafted a document warning of this danger and claiming that as a Christian one is bound to Christ, not by citizenship but by faith. (To read the full document one can go to www.cacn.org/statement.)

The only way forward for this nation is to embrace our diversity and recognize the gifts which people of every race, creed, and culture bring that make the rich tapestry called America. We are richer and stronger for the contributions of all of our citizens, no matter what their country of origin and no matter what their political or religious perspective. To denigrate or dismiss the value of anyone because of the color of their skin or their beliefs is in itself unpatriotic. We were founded as a nation of immigrants and prided ourselves on being a "melting pot" for the world. At one time we even believed the inscription on the Statue of Liberty, from the "New Colossus," written by Emma Lazarus: "Give me your tired, your poor, your huddled masses yearning to breathe free, the wretched refuse of your teeming shore. Send these, the homeless, tempest-tossed to me. I lift my lamp beside the golden door."[11] Perhaps we will once again embrace this sentiment.

WAY NINE:
Understand the Path of Hate that Leads to Genocide

Prejudice and hate toward others can spiral out of control and sometimes leads to Genocide as the "Progression of Hate" diagram shows.[12]

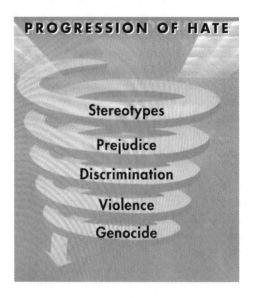

Genocide is the intentional effort to destroy a group of people in whole or in part. It is when one race or ethnic group that sees itself as superior to others chooses to dismiss and even eradicate those who are different and considered inferior. Those who advocate "White Supremacy" in this country, and others, embrace such tactics. Genocide is a process that develops over ten stages; and at each stage, preventive measures can stop it. The reason we have included it in this chapter, is to help the reader be aware of the process, be attuned to what actions of individuals or groups may be contributing to it and consider how to prevent it from happening. The process is not linear as some stages may occur simultaneously. Identified by Gregory Stanton, president of Genocide Watch, the ten stages are summarized below:

1. **Classification:** People are divided into "us and them"—German or Jew, Hutu or Tutsi, the list goes on.
2. **Symbolization:** We name people "Kikes" (Jews) or "Gypsies" and force symbols on them like the yellow star for Jews under Nazi rule.

3. **Discrimination:** People begin to face systematic discrimination. A dominant group uses the law to deny other people their rights. For example, the Nuremberg Laws of 1935 in Nazi Germany stripped German Jews of their citizenship.
4. **Dehumanization:** One group denies the humanity of another group. People equated with animals, vermin, or diseases.
5. **Organization:** The government creates specific groups (e.g., police, military, militias, ICE) to enforce these policies.
6. **Polarization:** The government broadcasts propaganda to turn the populace against a group. People are targeted if they speak up. Protesters may be labeled as traitors.
7. **Preparation:** Officials make plans to remove and relocate people considered undesirable. They also indoctrinate the public with fear about the victim group.
8. **Persecution:** The government begins to confiscate property of undesirable people and segregate them into ghettos or concentration camps. This happened in the United States to people of Japanese descent during WWII.
9. **Extermination:** This involves the wholesale elimination of a group. It is "extermina-tion" and not murder because the people are not considered human. Sometimes genocide will result in revenge killings by one group against another.
10. **Denial:** The government denies that it has committed any crime. Officials may try to cover up evidence and intimidate or discredit witnesses.[13]

America seems hopelessly divided today with hateful political rhetoric and fearmongering accelerating a sense of urgency. Radical groups are using the internet to stir up discontent and encourage persecution of certain groups. The nation is in danger of moving from stage eight to stage nine (extermination) much like what happened in Germany in the 1940s and more recently in places like Bosnia and Rwanda. We need civic and religious leaders who can bring us back from the brink by serving as healers rather than agitators, by seeking to unite us rather than divide us.

WAY TEN:
Never Stop Loving

How did a nation of immigrants come to hate immigrants, to fear and despise those who are different? Given our history and today's political climate, it is perhaps not a mystery. Yet to continue following that path is to turn our backs on our rich and diverse heritage.

Love can help us find our way. We need to be reminded about the importance of decency, honesty, and compassion. Recently, an attorney in the red state of Kentucky felt compelled to write an editorial on love and civility for a Lexington newspaper. His words ring true:

> We must change our approach to the issues now dividing us. We must stop digging in our heels for our position without a care for the other side. Instead we should see these issues as opportunities to build unity. . . . We must be eager to learn the other's viewpoint, empathize, and work for win/win compromises. Above all, we must strive for civility and treat others as we want to be treated.
>
> This "love" is nothing new for America's democracy. Our nation's laws, starting with the Constitution on down, are infused with "love," developed only after open dialogues of competing interests leading to compromise. Love is what keeps our nation United. Whether for families or our nation, love truly is the only real path to peace, joy, and freedom for all.[14]

In the past, America has been known for its compassion, generosity, tolerance, and openness. We must again embrace these core values—values that we find at the heart of most if not all of the world's religious teachings. And perhaps the most important lesson of all is that we are to practice love for our neighbor—whoever they may be and wherever they have come from.

This nation has endured two hundred and forty years of struggle, battling for the ideal "that we are all created equal" over against the sentiment that one race should rule over others. Every generation of Americans has attempted to open the door wider and wider for more people. Yet as the country approached the 2020 elections, the drumbeat for White Supremacy seemed to threaten to close those doors. In the summer of 2019, a self-proclaimed white nationalist targeted the Mexican population of El Paso, murdering twenty-two at a Walmart. It was the largest terrorist attack on Hispanic people in US history. To justify himself, the gunman cited a political manifesto that warned of an Hispanic invasion at the country's southern borders, encouraging hatred and violence against people of color.

What was unexpected was the way the community of El Paso came together in support of each other, much like Charleston in the aftermath of the shooting at Mother Emanuel four years earlier. In addition, the community of Juarez, Mexico—on the other side of the border—held a prayer vigil for the victims. Illuminated by candles and cell phones, people gathered at the barricade between the two countries praying and singing hymns in solidarity with their Hispanic sisters and brothers.

One family who had lost a father and grandfather was asked if they were angry and wanted revenge against the accused. They responded, "We choose to focus on love, forgiveness, and healing. We hope he finds God, because God takes us to love, not hate." They were living their faith, taking to heart what Jesus said in his Sermon on the Mount: "You have heard that it was said, 'You shall love your neighbor and hate your enemy.' But I say to you, Love your enemies and pray for those who persecute you, so that you may be children of your Father in heaven" (Matthew 5:43–45).

A Vision for the Future

The only positive future for America is one that embraces all of its diversity. Surely God desires us to be an inclusive nation rather than an exclusive one. And one way to achieve that goal is to continue to build bridges of understanding among people by encouraging multicultural and inter-religious relationships.

Perhaps we can find courage and inspiration in the words used by Senator Edward Kennedy to eulogize his brother, Senator Robert Kennedy, following his assassination:

> Our future may lie beyond our vision, but it is not completely beyond our control. It is the shaping impulse of America that neither fate nor nature nor the irresistible tides of history, but the work of our own hands, matched to reason and principle that will determine our destiny. There is pride in that, even arrogance, but there is also experience and truth. In any event, it is the only way we can live. . . .
>
> My brother need not be idealized, or enlarged in death beyond what he was in life; to be remembered simply as a good and decent man, who saw wrong and tried to right it, saw suffering and tried to heal it, saw war and tried to stop it. . . . Those of us who loved him and who take him to his rest today, pray that what he was to us and what he wished for others will someday come to pass for all the world. As he said many times, in many parts of this nation, to those he touched and who sought to touch him. As my brother often said: "Some men see things as they are and say why. I dream things that never were and say why not."[15]

We are at a turning point in American history. Will we choose to continue down a path toward exclusion, bigotry, hatred, and fear? Or can we as a nation summon our better angels and reclaim some of the basic human values of goodness, inclusion, fairness, love, forgiveness, humility, compassion, and justice? To ensure a vital, healthy, and life-giving future, America must rediscover its moral compass and find a spiritual center where the highest value is love of neighbor—be they citizen or non-citizen—and where everyone is considered a person of worth. The world is about to turn, and the question is which direction will we go? Perhaps we will choose to discover and celebrate the rich kaleidoscope that is America.

Questions for Reflection

1. What do you think of the statement, "The world cannot abide those who both condemn evil and envision a better future"? How is this true or not true?

2. If you were to prioritize the Ten Ways Forward that are described in this chapter, which two or three would you consider the most important?

3. Are there other "ways forward" that you can think of?

4. Are there opportunities in your community for engaging in multicultural or inter-religious dialogue? How might one go about starting such a conversation?

5. What do you think is God's vision for America's future? Describe your hope and dream.

Epilogue

Democracy is not a state. It is an act, and each generation
    must do its part
To help build what we called the Beloved Community, a
    nation and world
Society at peace with itself. Ordinary people with
    extraordinary vision can
Redeem the soul of America by getting in what I call good
    trouble.

      —John Lewis, Civil Rights Leader and Congressman
      From an essay written shortly before his death
      on July 17, 2020

The United States is among many nations across the globe that are reeling from the disastrous effects of the COVID-19 pandemic as this book goes to press. There are hopeful signs that this worldwide crisis may be bringing people closer together, even as they have practiced "social distancing." Perhaps some of the walls that have divided us are beginning to crumble as we recognize our common humanity, our equal vulnerability, and our need to rely on the kindnesses of one another. Compassionate examples have been sited of people checking in on their elderly neighbors and offering to pick-up groceries for them, of homemade masks being freely distributed to those on the front line, and of an increase in donations to food banks around the country.

At the same time, some of the divisions remain. While most mainline religious denominations chose to cease face-to-face gatherings in favor of online worship, some far right and independent faith leaders chose to defy state orders during mandatory lockdown, claiming that their right to religious freedom eclipsed exposing worshippers to the deadly virus. Politicians and others likewise used the crisis to point fingers at one another, often expending more energy at trying to establish blame than finding ways to work in harmony to meet its challenges.

Especially troubling have been armed vigilantes and crowds showing up at state capitals around the country, demanding that governors "open up" their states and allow people to return to work. Urged on by the president, they wave signs that say, "Fear the Government not COVID-19" or "Give me liberty or give me death," suggesting that their personal freedom and the economy is more important than lives that will likely be lost should the virus spike as a result. Where does this notion come from that individual rights are more important than the common good?

Ron Dreher believes that America is now governed by the idea that the individual has a right to make his or her own moral choices, and that personal freedom is cherished above all else. He writes:

> A virtuous society, by contrast, is one that shares belief in objective moral good and the practices necessary for human beings to embody those goods in [and for the sake of] community. To live 'after virtue,' then, is to dwell in a society that not only can no longer agree on what constitutes virtuous belief and conduct but also doubts that virtue exists. In a post-virtue society, individuals hold maximal freedom of thought and action.[1]

Society, then, becomes a group of individuals where everyone simply pursues their own interests and does what they think is right for them without concern for others.

A 1793 slogan born out of the French Revolution has become that country's national motto: "*liberté, egalité, fraternité*"—liberty, equality, fraternity. This puts the idea of freedom in the context of community (brotherhood) and equality for all. We believe this is what the founders of our nation intended when the constitution and Bill of Rights were written. And now in a time a national crisis, we are given the opportunity to reclaim this ideal. This is not a time for partisan politics but for national unity. In a short video message shared on a number of social media platforms in early May of 2020, former President George W. Bush urged Americans to come together in the face of a shared threat. "In the final analysis, we are not partisan combatants, we are human beings, equally vulnerable and equally wonderful in the sight of God," Bush said. "We rise or fall together, and we are determined to rise."[2]

Times of stress and fear cause many people to demonize the "other" and, in worst cases, attack them. For example, the country has seen an alarming rise in violent crimes against Asians since the outbreak, much like the rise in hate crimes against Muslims after 9/11. The Trump administration has helped fan the flames of bigotry by insisting China is to blame for the pandemic and the resulting world crisis. Furthermore, on March 25, 2020, US Secretary of State Mike Pompeo encouraged foreign ministers from the G7 (Group of 7 leading industrialized democracies) to use the term "Wuhan Virus." And the campaign to re-elect President Trump soon after released a video wrongly identifying Gary Locke (who is Chinese American and a former US ambassador to China) as a Chinese official. Locke's response was swift: "There is one priority that matters in America right now: stopping this virus and saving lives. So I have no tolerance for the same old politics of distraction and division. We need leaders who understand we can only get through this crisis together—as Americans of every creed, color, and background."[3]

We find ourselves in one of the most pivotal moments in recent US history. Individuals and organizations are facing circumstances that lead to new ways of thinking, behaving, and understanding who we are. Not only is the pandemic changing behavior but the tsunami of "Black Lives Matter" demonstrations—in response to the wrongful death of George Floyd and other African American men—has ignited a healthy debate regarding racism and police brutality in this country. The initial response to the protests has been swift and surprising in statements of solidarity issued by religious leaders and organizations, in pledges made by corporations to change products and behavior, in the removal of Confederate statues from public places, and even in Nascar banning images of the Confederate flag at all racing events.

What is different this time is the public support for systemic change. "In 2011, only 21 percent of white Americans said 'racism in our society' was a big problem. By 2015, that number had climbed to 43. Now it's 60. In 2016, only 26 percent of white respondents expressed a favorable opinion of the Black Lives Matter movement. Two years later, 36 percent did. Now 51 percent do. In 2015, 45 percent of white respondents said 'racial and ethnic discrimination in the United States' was a big problem. By 2016, that number had risen to 64. Now it's 71."[4] One can hope that our corporate conscience has been awakened to the point where real and positive change may be possible.

Perhaps there is a silver lining to all of this. It might be that the common enemy of a pandemic may be the catalyst that brings us together. Polls show that the country—despite our differences—is more united than any time since 9/11. Columnist David Brooks comments on the fact that the pandemic has been a stark reminder of our mutual interdependence as well as the need for a strong, effective government. He writes: "The pandemic has been a massive humanizing force—allowing us to see each other on a level much deeper than politics—see the fragility, the fear and the courage. . . . We're also being united by those who are sacrificing for the common good." He concludes: "Americans have responded to this [crisis] with more generosity and solidarity than we had any right to expect. . . . The job ahead is to make this unity last."[5]

For a time such as this, we need to come together as a nation and as a global community. We need to emulate the spirit expressed by the Big Cities Health Coalition when they published a statement in newspapers across the country that ended with this plea: "While we ask you to stay apart physically, we implore you to come together emotionally and spiritually. *Together* we are the best defense against this pandemic."[6] It is our hope that this book will be one of the resources that can provide healing and help restore the common good.

Appendix 1:
Litany of Confession for
The Day of Mourning

Introduction

The Day of Mourning Worship Resource[1]—endorsed by the Fifteenth Assembly of the Uniting Church in Australia at the request of the Uniting Aboriginal and Islander Christian Congress (UAICC)—reminds us of the dispossession and violence against First Nation People. It invites Christians to stand together in remembering the truth of our history and honoring the culture of those First Peoples, their families, and the next generations. *In the liturgy that follows, the light text is spoken by the worship leader and the congregation responds with the bold text.*

Call to Worship

Our land is alive with the glory of God;
    desert sands hum and gum trees dance.
Brown grasses sing
    and mountains breathe their stillness.
All created things add their rhythms of delight
    and even stones rap out their praise.
Let our voices mingle with those of the earth;
    may our hearts join the beat of her joy,
    for our triune God is with us:
    the Source of all being surrounds and upholds us.
    Christ Jesus walks beside and before us.
The Spirit moves within and between us.
Blessed be God, our wonder and delight.
Acknowledgement of First Peoples
    Today, as we gather to worship,
    we acknowledge the peoples,
    the first inhabitants of this place
    from time beyond remembering.
We acknowledge that through this land,
    God nurtured and sustained the First Peoples of this country,
    the Aboriginal and Islander peoples.
We honor them for their custodianship

of the land on which we gather today.
We acknowledge that the First Peoples
  had already encountered the Creator God
  before the arrival of the colonizers;
  the Spirit was already in the land,
  revealing God to the people
  through law, custom and ceremony.
We acknowledge that the same love and grace
  that was finally and fully revealed in Jesus Christ
  sustained the First Peoples
  and gave them particular insights into God's ways;
  and so we rejoice in the reconciling purposes of God
  found in the good news about Jesus Christ.

OR

We acknowledge the Clan/Nation
  the sovereign First Peoples of this place.
We honor their elders past and present
  together with all descendants of this Nation,
  for their care for these lands and waters since creation.

Greeting

Today friends, we are remembering the tragic history of our nation and the
  violent dispossession of her First Peoples. Today is a Day of Mourning.
  Today we mark in lament the truth of our shared history and we lift up to
  God our prayers for First Peoples and our nation.
We say sorry and we pray for forgiveness, healing and hope. But today is also
  a day
of worship. So we come together and give thanks to God for the abundant
  grace and liberating hope which we know through Jesus Christ and which
  is for all people.
The God of all justice, the God of all peace, be with you all.
And also with you.

Invocation

Abba, Father, Bäpa[2] God, source of all life, answer our call,
as a mother responds to the cry of a child in the night.
Jesus Christ, brother and friend, Liberator, stand beside us
as bearer of our humanity, and sharer of God's grace.
Creator Spirit, giver of new life, purposeful guest, prod us to praise,
calling us to be a people of hope and faith in Christ Jesus.
Amen.

Lament and Confession

Merciful God, we, the Second Peoples of this land, acknowledge and lament the injustice and abuse that has so often marked the treatment of the First Peoples of this land.

We acknowledge and lament the way in which their land was taken from them and their language, culture, law and spirituality despised and suppressed.

We acknowledge and lament the way in which the Christian church was so often not only complicit in this process but actively involved in it.

We acknowledge and lament that in our own time the injustice and abuse has continued.

We have been indifferent when we should have been outraged, we have been apathetic when we should have been active, we have been silent when we should have spoken out.

Liberating Jesus, hear our lament and by your Spirit bring healing, hope and transformation to the lives of our First Nations sisters and brothers and their communities, we pray.

Gracious God, hear our acknowledgments —We have not loved you with our whole heart, nor have we loved First Peoples and other neighbors as ourselves.

God of mercy, forgive us for our failures, past and present and give us the grace today to make a fresh start.

By your Spirit transform our minds and hearts so that we may love as you have loved us,that we may boldly speak your truth and courageously do your will.

Through Jesus Christ our Lord. Amen.

Declaration of Forgiveness

This is the best of all:

When we are empty, God fills us;
when we are disheartened, God is compassionate;
when we are wounded, God brings healing;
when we confess our sin, God forgives.

In Christ, through Christ and because of Christ,
our sins are forgiven.
Thanks be to God.
You refill the cup of life, O God.
In Christ, we find refuge, strength and hope.
Amen.

Appendix 2:
A Liturgy of Repentance and Reconciliation

Prepared by Evangelical Lutheran Church in Canada in Collaboration with the Indigenous People of Canada[1]

Introduction

This rite of confession is the result of a very honest and powerful conversation with tribal members of the Regina Indigenous Christian Fellowship regarding broken relationships and the need for healing. This liturgy is commended to congregations as part of their own journey toward reconciliation.

Confession

When we listen to the stories of Indigenous people who lived on this land long before people imagined you could own land, we hear of a people with an ethic of caring for the land to the seventh generation.

> We hear of a people who strove to live in deep relationship with the land,
> **the creatures of the land, and the whole creation.**
> And now... our scientists tell us of a global crisis that includes
> **Rising Global Temperature faster than expected in Canada,**
> **Widespread Melting of Arctic Sea Ice,**
> **Changing precipitation patterns,**
> **Changes in frequency and intensity of extreme weather events**
> **Millions of people facing displacement ...**
> **We confess that we have not cared for the earth and our neighbors.**
> **We are reacting too slowly to the global climate crisis.**
> **We have forgotten that we are called to be stewards of creation**
> **We are too invested in economic stability and unsustainable lifestyles and**
> **have much fear.**
> **Forgive us for what we have done and we have left undone. And so we repent.**

When we listen to our treaty partners in Canada, we hear stories of ongoing struggle and hurt. We are told of the effects of residential schools and the intergenerational violence that occurs as one generation passes the hurt and abuse to next.

> We hear a deep lament about how profoundly daily living is dragged down by
> the scars of old wounds which are all too often ripped open by new damage.

We hear that in our rush to recognize the hurts of the past and to quickly move forward we often fail to understand the full depth of the hurt that individuals and families experienced and how this permanent damage continues to express itself today.

We hear that there is much difficult work and healing yet to come.

We confess that we have looked away when confronted with the suffering of our Indigenous neighbors.

We have been reluctant to call on governments to fulfill treaty obligations.

We have sought quick solutions and watched government public apologies that failed to restore equity and did not bring healing.

Forgive us where we have been inwardly turned to our own needs and failed to be open to the ongoing suffering of our Indigenous neighbors. And so we repent

When we listen we hear that stripping people of their culture is stripping them of their personhood.

We hear that in being colonized and systematically pushed out of the way, the stories and gifts of the Indigenous community are not heard or given value.

We hear that colonization worked out as planned. . . . So much of the Indigenous ways of knowing were taken away . . . entire languages have been lost, and new western values and ways have been installed.

We hear a deep lament that the richness of our treaty partners' culture was dismissed as second class.

We hear that colonial ways of evaluating personal worth and personal success were imposed.

We confess that we have been arrogant in judging and demeaning the wisdom and beauty of Indigenous culture. We have imposed our culture on others and we forgot that all people reflect the image of God.

We confess that we have not been good treaty partners.

We have avoided learning our own Canadian history.

We have ignored the difficulties and hurts our forbearers have caused in assuming that our way of knowing and being was always the best. And so we repent.

When we listen we hear that we did not often understand or respect what the first peoples of this land already knew about how to live . . . how to nurture and value creation.

We hear how the land wants to care for the people and has much goodness to give.

We hear of the massacre of the millions of buffalo that once roamed here.

We hear that the pursuit of land and wealth hurt and displaced 1000s of communities.

We confess that we did not see and hear how the First Nations respected the sacredness of the land. We did not join them in the work of the Creator's call to stewardship.

We confess that we have ignored the cries of the pain as settlement and displacement is the history we share. And so we repent.

When we listen we hear that all people are weary of the work that healing the past requires.

We hear that healing is coming but full healing takes time, patience and understanding.

We hear that when someone says "get over it" and someone else says "I'm tired of doing this apology again" it belittles the reality of the deep wounds that colonization has inflicted on people and creation.

We hear that all people must keep working at being in good relationship and make space for the healing to keep coming.

We confess that we do not always seek relationships.

We do not always seek peace.

We do not always make space for reconciliation and grieving.

We do not make space for healing. And so we repent.

Absolution

Family of God in Christ, we long for a time when we have finished our walk together through the healing hours of the night . . . where we will together dance in the joy that comes in the morning.

The Creator hears the cries of the people.

God in infinite grace reaches out to all with forgiveness, healing and hope.

God is working reconciliation among us.

In the Creator's name & by the Creator's command I proclaim God's forgiveness to us all.

May we rise from the dust of our sorrow, be filled with the Spirit of reconciliation and engage the work of the church here and now and this convention of the Evangelical Lutheran Church In Canada . . . in Regina Saskatchewan. . . . In the homeland of the Métis where first of many covenantal treaties were signed—we are on blessed to share and be on Treaty 4 territory.

Where once we were people of stopped ears may we now hear.

Where once we were people with hearts of stone may we become broken open.

Where once we were people turned in on ourselves may we work for community and reconciliation.

Where once we were weary let us rise up on the wings of eagles and work out our faith.

Amen.

Appendix 3:
Declaration of the ELCA
to People of African Descent

On June 27, 2019, the Church Council of the Evangelical Lutheran Church in America adopted the following declaration as a statement addressed to people of African descent. Affirmed by the voting members of the Churchwide Assembly meeting in Milwaukee in August 2019.[1]

There is no longer Jew or Greek, there is no longer slave or free, there is no longer male and female; for all of you are one in Christ Jesus. (Galatians 3:28)

The Evangelical Lutheran Church in America (ELCA) apologizes to people of African descent for its historical complicity in slavery and its enduring legacy of racism in the United States and globally. We lament the white church's failure to work for the abolition of slavery and the perpetuation of racism in this church. We confess, repent and repudiate the times when this church has been silent in the face of racial injustice.

The ELCA acknowledges that slavery created and perpetuated racism, a truth this nation and this church have yet to fully embrace. The enslavement of Africans was based on a false narrative of the racial inferiority and the demonization of black people by the majority culture. Slavery was supported by white religious, legal, political, and scientific leaders and institutions for social, political, and economic gain. During the 246-year transatlantic slave trade, which began in 1619, an estimated 12 million people from Africa were stolen from their native lands, separated from their families, torn from their culture, killed for seeking freedom, tortured through inhumane forms of punishment, and subjected to lifetimes of captivity. While the white church stood silently by, people of African descent resisted through acts of rebellion, created new expressions of spirituality and Christian practice rooted in African traditions, and organized movements for freedom.

The ELCA teaches that racism is sin and that racism denies the reconciling work of the cross.[2] Rooted in slavery, racism is manifested through the history of Jim Crow policies, racial segregation, the terror of lynching, extrajudicial killings by law enforcement, and the disproportionate incarceration of people of color.[3] Descendants of formerly enslaved Africans are still denied equal access and opportunity in church and society while white people collectively benefit from unequal access, opportunity, and power. Institutional racism currently exists in the ELCA through discriminatory treatment within the call process; inequitable compensation of clergy of color; racial segregation; divestment from black communities and congregations; systemic polices and organizational practices; and failure to fully include the gifts of leadership and worship styles of people of African descent.

The ELCA trusts that repentance begins and ends with the work of a gracious God. In prayerful response to the African Descent Lutheran Association's request for an apology, this church enters into a season of confession and lamentation. Beyond empty promises or well-meaning intentions, this church recommits to the work of racial justice, socioeconomic equity, and racial reconciliation. This apology is a recommitment to the process of right and equitable relations within this church, and the flourishing of Christ's church universal.

This recommitment means working toward a deeper understanding of slavery and its legacy, of institutional and structural racism, of white privilege, and of attitudes and foundations of white supremacy. It means praying for the renewal of this church as disciples of the living Christ.

Why Is the ELCA Issuing this Apology?

In 2015, the African Descent Lutheran Association (ADLA) called the ELCA 2016 Churchwide Assembly (CWA) to "draft a formal letter of repentance," to commit to examine the church's complicity in slavery, and to acknowledge "the ELCA's perpetuation of racism." This call was founded in the ELCA's 1993 social statement *Freed in Christ: Race, Ethnicity, and Culture*, which confessed the sin of racism, defined this sin as "a mix of power, privilege, and prejudice," and acknowledged that "skin color makes a difference" and that "white people benefit from a privileged position" as "we fall back into enslaving patterns of injustice."[4]

In response, the assembly adopted social policy resolution CA 16.04.17, which resolves:

- To confess and repent of the Lutheran church's complicity in four hundred years of enslavement, oppression, and marginalization of African-descent people and other marginalized populations;

- To acknowledge with regret that the ELCA as an institution has and continues to contribute to racial harassment and discrimination against people of African descent through corporate action, policy, and practices; and

- To request that the Domestic Mission unit, through its African Descent Ministries desk and in consultation with the African Descent Lutheran Association, create

- "Declaration of the ELCA to the African Descent Community" and to bring this declaration, along with recommendations for how to include it in this church's governing documents, to the April 2018 meeting of the ELCA's Church Council.

The ELCA is issuing this apology alongside the Lutheran World Federation's "Resolution on Commemorating the 2019 Quad-centennial of the Forced Transatlantic Voyage of Enslaved African Peoples to the Americas—Human Beings Not for Sale!," adopted at the LWF Council meeting in Geneva, Switzerland, June 13-18, 2019. That resolution reads in part:

> This year [2019] is the 400th anniversary of the forced transatlantic voyage of enslaved African peoples. The transatlantic slave trade impacted peoples in major regions of the world, including Africa, Europe, and the Americas.
>
> The transatlantic slave trade, which ripped enslaved African peoples away from their rich traditions, histories, and assets, led to systematic oppression of people of African descent in the United States and globally; colonial and post-colonial policies; racist beliefs, policies, and practices; imbalances of privilege, power, and wealth; and the continuing demand for low or no-wage labor which are manifestations of the legacy of slavery.
>
> The global ecumenical family, of which the LWF and its member churches are a part, is commemorating the 400th anniversary and engaging in work to address the legacy of slavery, the sin of racism, and the epidemic of human trafficking as part of the UN Decade in Solidarity with People of African Descent 2015–2024.

Why Look at Slavery? It Happened in the Past

Slavery and its legacy inform our concept of race and the modern state of race relations in the United States. Race is a social construct with no basis in biology; it took shape in the United States through a process that assigned meaning to physical differences for social, political, and economic purposes. The idea of race was defined by scientists in the 1700s as they developed categories of human species and was cemented in the U.S. through the institution of slavery, with a hierarchy of whites as superior and blacks as inferior. The following laws and actions from the 1600s demonstrate how the idea of race was constructed and how it was used to benefit persons identified as white and to enslave people of African descent.

1619 Twenty people from Africa are brought to Jamestown, Virginia, and sold into slavery.

1640 Servitude for life is established, separating people by race into white and black. John Punch, a runaway black indentured servant, is sentenced to servitude for life; his two white indentured companions are sentenced to seven years of service.

1641 Massachusetts becomes the first colony to legalize slavery; others soon follow.

1662 Slavery becomes hereditary with a Virginia law that children born to an enslaved mother inherit her status.

1664 Maryland mandates lifelong servitude for all enslaved blacks, with other colonies to follow.

1667 Virginia declares that Christian baptism will not alter a person's status as a slave; other colonies follow with similar laws.

1676 Bacon's Rebellion includes enslaved blacks and both black and white indentured servants. Laws passed in its wake discriminate by race, abolishing enslaved people's rights to bear arms, congregate in groups, testify in court, move around without a pass, and learn to read English, and permitting masters to kill an enslaved person during punishment.

Slavery and land stolen from indigenous peoples were firmly established in the British colonies as an economic system and were used to build a new nation and increase individual wealth. George Washington, the first US president, owned up to 200 enslaved people. Thomas Jefferson, the third president and a wealthy slave-owner, argued in his *Notes on the State of Virginia* "that blacks were inferior to whites in reason and imagination: 'This unfortunate difference of colour [sic], and perhaps of faculty, is a powerful obstacle to the emancipation of these people.'"[5] The US Constitution, adopted in 1787, included a Fugitive Slave Clause that allowed slaves, including those from "free states," to be returned to their owners; it also provided for the US Census to count each slave as three-fifths of a person.

• • •

Politically and economically, the new nation was built on the backs of enslaved people of African descent, along with other people of color, while continuing to establish the rights and supremacy of whites. In 1790, the Naturalization Act denied naturalization to anyone who was not a free white, and the 1857 Supreme Court ruling on *Dred Scott v. Sandford* denied citizenship to all slaves, ex-slaves, and descendants of slaves. Under President Andrew Jackson, voting rights were expanded to include all white males over the age of 21, firmly establishing the benefit of whiteness. As the Civil War ended and slavery was abolished in 1865 with the Thirteenth Amendment to the Constitution, four million enslaved people were freed. That freedom, however, was short-lived as new forms of oppression took shape.

Slavery Is Over, So Why Can't We Just Move On?

While the Thirteenth Amendment promised to end slavery as it was then known, the amendment's provisions allowed slavery or involuntary servitude as punishment for crimes[6] and thereby allowed slavery to be rebuilt in another form, first through convict leasing in the years following the Civil War and more recently through tough-on-crime policies and mass incarceration, which have disproportionately impacted people of African descent and other persons of color. As Michelle Alexander writes in her book *The New Jim Crow*:

Like Jim Crow (and slavery), mass incarceration operates as a tightly networked system of laws, policies, customs, and institutions that operate collectively to ensure the subordinate status of a group defined largely by race.[7]

The ELCA social statement *The Church and Criminal Justice: Hearing the Cries* (2013) states, "The ELCA believes that present criminal justice practices and legislation have produced blatantly unacceptable results with respect to race."[8]

Race, as it was constructed through 245 years of enslavement, therefore continued to take on meaning and impact after the abolishment of slavery. Images, stereotypes, laws, and practices defined the political, economic, and social oppression of people of African descent. The 1915 film *The Birth of a Nation* portrayed black men as dangerous, unintelligent, and sexually aggressive toward white women. Those images were used to instill fear and to maintain social separation of people defined as white and black. Black Codes were enacted immediately after the Civil War to limit the freedom of people of African descent and to ensure the continuation of a cheap labor force through sharecropping and the accumulation of debt. Jim Crow laws were enacted to legalize separation of whites and blacks, with the 1896 Supreme Court case *Plessy v. Ferguson* enshrining "separate but equal" as a legal principle. During the 90 years of Jim Crow and sixty years of "separate but equal," more than four thousand black people were publicly lynched in the United States in acts of terror.[9]

Meanwhile, free from oppressive and restrictive laws, white people benefited politically, socially, and economically. White people and white systems continued to exert power and superiority through practices of harassment and intimidation, redlining and denial of loans, restrictive covenants for housing, restrictions of voting rights, white flight, and lack of access to good schools, transportation systems, and jobs. The institution of slavery ended in 1865, but its legacy has continued to do harm in "how economic forces work against people of color in housing, medical care, education, and employment."[10]

Slavery Ended Over 150 Years Ago, and I Am a White Lutheran Who Never Owned Slaves. How and Why Am I a Part of This Apology?

In the United States, people identified as white benefit from their skin color whether or not they're descended from a slave-owning family, whether they're recent immigrants or their ancestors have been in this country for several generations, and whether they come from an upper or lower socioeconomic class. The timeline and examples above show that racial systems have been constructed throughout history and have given social, economic, and political meaning to racial identities. In 1988, writer Peggy McIntosh expanded the understanding of white privilege as she developed a list of advantages enjoyed by white people simply because of skin color.

These privileges range from normalizing whiteness through regular items, such as fleshcolored Band-Aids, to seeing white people widely represented as having founded this country. Within the church, white and black worshippers were raised with images and stained-glass windows of a white Jesus and white disciples, and generally accepted these depictions as fact. In school, teachers and textbooks taught that the inventors, scientists, writers, and artists who built this country were primarily white.

"As white people in the United States, we each have our personal stories that may make privilege difficult to see," writes Joyce Caldwell in "Troubling the Waters for Healing of the Church."

> Too often we hear in ourselves—and in others—that we are not racist. We are not privileged. After all, we may have grown up with few resources, and we have generally all worked for what we have. What we fail to see is that we have a moving platform (as in the airports) of privilege making our path easier. I grew up on a farm. We had few resources. I was poorer than many of the young people in my high school. I didn't see I had advantages. I worked hard in education and jobs. But then I have to look hard at the log in my own eye. I have to look at the chains of privilege and know that I am White.
>
> I benefit. I am privileged. My ancestors were able to vote; to obtain loans and build ownership; to have access to the schools and colleges of choice; to choose where to live. Those benefits accrue through the generations. Despite differences of socio-economic class, white skin provides a benefit in and of itself.[11]

Unearned privilege runs deep, and white people can't escape it. It is not based on individual attitudes or behavior. Racism is a system of structural advantage. The concept of race was built for political and economic advantage for those who are white at the expense of indigenous people and people of color. Enslavement of people of African descent provided the free labor that built the US Capitol building and many churches and university buildings, along with much of the wealth of the United States.

What Is the History of Lutherans Related to Slavery?

Although the practice of slavery was legal, it was morally and ethically wrong. The ELCA has defined racism as sin, but that acknowledgement requires examination of complicity in slavery. Writer R. M. Chapman examines three responses among Lutherans prior to the Civil War—slave-owning, antislavery, and quietism.[12] While Lutherans entered the debate on slavery relatively late compared to other denominations, in 1862, the General Synod split between North and South over the issue of slavery. Lutherans in southern states had been slaveholders since at least the 1730s. In the years leading up to and through the Civil War, southern

Lutherans defended slavery and white racial superiority, supporting their positions with Scripture.

Some Lutherans in the South questioned the morality of slavery, along with Lutherans in the North. The Franckean Synod of New York was the most vocal in taking an abolitionist stance and rebuking slavery as sin. "On the whole, Lutherans did not become strong anti-slavery advocates, nor did they champion the cause of free blacks in the North or the South."[13] Lutherans were complicit in slavery as they largely stood by in passively accepting the practice as the law of the land. With much of the Lutheran church's history and emphasis on being an immigrant church, Lutherans as a whole remained on the sidelines through the Jim Crow years and much of the civil rights era and subsequent years, with pockets of advocacy and political action.

What Is the History of People of African Descent in Resilience and Resistance?

Since the beginning of the enslavement of people of African descent in 1619 and through the 245 years of chattel slavery, people of African descent resisted their oppression, through rebellions, running away, and day-to-day actions.[14] Nat Turner's rebellion in 1831 is well known, but collectively all rebellions, whether or not they were able to be executed, demonstrated the will of those who were enslaved to end the dehumanizing and morally corrupt institution of slavery. Enslaved persons also resisted and sought their freedom through running away, with Harriet Tubman alone helping more than two hundred people escape to freedom. For those who could not escape, resistance came through day-to-day actions played out against their workload and the property of their masters.

In 1857, Frederick Douglass, a former slave and an ardent abolitionist and supporter of women's rights, noted the important role that the resistance of the oppressed plays in awakening the conscience and morality of both the government and the church:

> For a long time [slaveholders] have taught our Congress, and Senate, and Pulpits, what subjects should be discussed, and what objects should command our attention. . . . This struggle may be a moral one, or it may be a physical one, and it may be both moral and physical, but it must be a struggle. Power concedes nothing without a demand. It never did and it never will.[15]

People of African descent continued to press for freedom in taking roles of government leadership in state houses and the US Congress during the years of Reconstruction; in establishing black colleges and universities; in continuing acts of resistance and calls for freedom during the Jim Crow era; in becoming skilled in the law to argue cases for freedom and equal treatment; and in standing up, sitting down, and raising voices and fists for freedom during the civil rights movement. The press for freedom continues in advocacy and action against mass incarceration and in the Black Lives Matter movement.

From the days of enslavement to the current day, the black church has been instrumental in providing a place for those facing oppression in daily life to hear words of hope and be engaged in communities of action. The voices of hope and resistance against injustice have been proclaimed in small prayer gatherings of enslaved people, from pulpits at Historical Black Churches, and from black pastors and predominately African American congregations in the ELCA. Those voices are present now in the call to renewed action from the African Descent Lutheran Association.

Where Do We Go from Here as a Church?

Recognizing the words of Frederick Douglass that "power concedes nothing without a demand," those who are white within the ELCA must listen to and follow the leadership of people of African descent in implementing the intent of "Declaration of the ELCA to People of African Descent."

The 2016 adopted social policy resolution "Renewed Action Regarding Racism Toward Lutherans of African Descent" (CA16.05.17) calls for a recommitment "to create, sustain and reinvest in African descent communities, congregations, and ministries" and to "recommit this church to growing its ethnic and racial diversity" in leadership, congregations, and communities.

In addition, the ELCA Church Council adopted the following actions on June 27, 2019:

• To call this church into a time of study and to support the apology by encouraging congregations, synods, and the churchwide organization to find ways to share this apology broadly;

• To encourage congregations, synods, and the churchwide organization to observe an annual Day of Repentance;

• To affirm the Lutheran World Federation Council resolution "Commemorating the 2019 Quad-centennial of the Forced Transatlantic Voyage of Enslaved African Peoples to the Americas—Human Beings Not for Sale!";

• To engage in anti-racism and racial justice work, work toward economic justice— including the study of reparations;

• To work to address and end modern forms of slavery and human trafficking (CC19.06.23).

An apology is only empty words and promises unless it is accompanied by action, which is grounded in prayer, education, and soul-searching repentance. We trust that God can make all things new.

Appendix 4:
A Declaration of Inter-Religious Commitment
A Policy Statement of the
Evangelical Lutheran Church in America [1]

Foreword: Historical Considerations

The Evangelical Lutheran Church in America (ELCA) has been engaging in inter-religious relations since its formation in 1988, building upon the legacy of its predecessor bodies, the work of The Lutheran World Federation (LWF), and the witness of our ecumenical partners.

As part of the global Lutheran communion, we wrestle with and lament Martin Luther's troubling legacy regarding inter-religious relations, especially his anti-Judaic and anti-Islamic writings. Importantly, the first major inter-religious witness of this church was the adoption of a "Declaration of the ELCA to the Jewish Community" (1994), which repudiated Luther's vile anti-Judaic diatribes and reached out in love and respect to the Jewish community.

Over the years, our inter-religious relations have deepened and expanded. As a church, we have developed educational resources, engaged in dialogue and common action, defended our neighbors against religious bigotry, and cared for our various partnerships. While we have focused on Jewish and Muslim relations, we have also participated in organizations and efforts that reflect the broader diversity of religions and worldviews in the United States and globally.

Our 1991 policy statement, "A Declaration of Ecumenical Commitment," called for "a separate, official statement" that would reflect the "distinct responsibility for the church to enter into conversations and reach deeper understanding with people of other faiths." This inter-religious policy statement seeks to fulfill this recommendation and complements our church's ecumenical policy statement.

Whenever possible, the ELCA cooperates with other Christians in building relations with those of other religions and worldviews. Councils of churches are an important avenue of dialogue and common action. While not all Christians are interested in or supportive of inter-religious relations, this commitment is receiving increased attention in many churches. Our Christian companions have greatly enhanced our journey. In fact, the inter-religious statements of our ecumenical partners have informed the development of this document.

At the same time, the ELCA has something distinctive to say about our inter-religious commitments. As a policy statement, this document provides a common framework for the diverse ministries of this church. The twelve commitments provide a succinct summary of the policy and may prove useful in certain contexts as a stand-alone aid. The afterword goes deeper into the biblical, confessional, and theological basis for the policy. As used in this document, the word "religion" refers to various forms of beliefs and practices, such as Buddhism, Confucianism, Hinduism, Islam, Judaism, Sikhism, Taoism, and traditional indigenous spiritualities. Whenever "neighbor" is used, it refers to all those who profess a religion, as well as those who do not, including those who consider themselves atheists or agnostics or ascribe to other worldviews that are not explicitly religious. "We" refers to the individual members and participants, as well as to the congregations and ministries of the whole church. This document seeks to address a Lutheran approach to understanding and engaging with our neighbors in a multi-religious, pluralistic context.

As descriptions of the teachings of other religions and worldviews are readily available elsewhere, this policy statement does not seek to explain or categorize them. Neither does it seek to provide a theology of world religions. Instead, its focus is on our dual calling to witness to Christ and to love our neighbor. As such, this document serves as an invitation to individuals, congregations, ministries, institutions, and expressions of the ELCA to engage constructively with our neighbors of other religions and worldviews. In this declaration, our neighbors may also find greater clarity about who we are, what they can expect of us, and why and how our Christian faith and Lutheran self-understanding compel us into dialogue and common action. In all of this, may greater understanding and cooperation throughout the *Oikoumene*—the whole inhabited earth—enhance the justice, peace, and life abundant that God intends for us all.

Introduction

As the ELCA, we enter into inter-religious relations on the basis of our Christian identity and Lutheran self-understanding. As we engage with our neighbors of other religions and worldviews, it is important that we clearly articulate who we are, what we believe, and why. "This church confesses Jesus Christ as Lord and Savior and the Gospel as the power of God for the salvation of all who believe" (ELCA Constitution, Chapter 2). As a confessional church, we understand ourselves to be evangelical, catholic, and A policy statement of the Evangelical Lutheran Church in America 3 ecumenical. "To be *evangelical* means to be committed to the Gospel of Jesus Christ. . . . To be *catholic* means to be committed to the fullness of the apostolic faith and its creedal, doctrinal articulation for the entire world. . . . To be *ecumenical* means to be committed to the oneness to which God calls the world in the saving gift of Jesus Christ" ("A Declaration of Ecumenical Commitment," 1991).

"Jesus Christ is the Word of God incarnate, through whom everything was made and through whose life, death, and resurrection God fashions a new creation" (ELCA Constitution, Chapter 2). This is the gospel—the good news of what God has done, is doing, and will do for all in Christ. It is a gift from God, freely given, without any requirements that need to be fulfilled. "Sharing the good news," or evangelism, is using words and deeds to pass this life-changing message along to others. We describe this as the work of the Great Commission (Matthew 28:19–20). As witnesses to the good news of Jesus Christ, we entrust to the Holy Spirit the work of turning that witness into faith. With the work of being a witness comes an invitation to love God and to love and serve the neighbor, which is known as the Great Commandment (Matthew 22:34–40). This neighborly response is not fueled simply by human kindness. We believe that God entrusts to us as "in clay jars" (2 Corinthians 4:7) the "message of reconciliation" for all (2 Corinthians 5:19). We believe that "Christ, our peace, has put an end to the hostility of race, ethnicity, gender, and economic class" ("Freed in Christ: Race, Ethnicity, and Culture," ELCA social statement, 1993, p. 1). In a deeply divided world, and as a faithful response to Christ's message of reconciliation, we seek right, peaceful, and just relationships with all our neighbors, including those of other religions and worldviews. We do this as an expression of our Christian faith, and as a continuation of the covenant God made with us in holy baptism "to serve all people, following the example of Jesus, and to strive for justice and peace in all the earth" (*Evangelical Lutheran Worship [ELW]*, Affirmation of Baptism).

Context

Our context, whether understood locally or globally, is multi-religious. Our Lutheran vocation both shapes *and* is shaped by our engagement with religious diversity.

Encountering Religious Diversity

Religious diversity has continually shaped American society, starting with the indigenous peoples of this land. Though many colonizers came to this land in search of religious freedom, they systematically and violently denied it to the indigenous peoples already here. We publicly confess this sin in our 2016 ELCA "Repudiation of the Doctrine of Discovery," which was an important step in a long path toward "repentance and reconciliation to native nations in this country for damage done in the name of Christianity."

Every chapter of US history has had a lasting impact on our identity as a religiously diverse nation. This includes our sinful history of slavery, as well as various waves of migration and immigration. In recent decades, this history, as well as new patterns of forced displacement and new kinds of religious affiliation, has resulted in rapid and radical changes to our multi-religious landscape. Christians in the United States are now more likely than in previous generations to encounter neighbors of other religions and worldviews in their communities, schools, workplaces, civic spaces, circles of friends, and families.

Responding to Our Context

As a church, we must consider anew our calling and commitments in a multi-religious world. Many Lutherans and Lutheran ministries already participate in inter-religious activities such as theological dialogue, advocacy, and service, which build mutual understanding and advance the common good, defined as justice and peace for all of creation. As Lutherans, we are called to move from mere coexistence to a more robust engagement. It is through authentic, mutual relationships that we can truly love our neighbors as people made in the image of God. This commitment includes confronting whenever possible the often-compounding oppressions experienced by people of various religions and worldviews on the basis of race, ethnicity, gender, and class.

Fear and Division

There are many ways individuals and communities can respond to religious difference. The most harmful responses are grounded in ignorance and fear, which can breed stereotypes. In the extreme, these responses can fuel incidents of religious bigotry, restrict religious freedoms, and arouse conflicts that are destructive of life, property, and the environment. We live in a context of ongoing anti-Muslim bigotry and anti-Semitism, as well as incidents of harassment and violence directed against these and other minority religious and ethnic communities. In some cases, the words and deeds of a few are used to discredit entire religious communities. Unfortunately, in every religion, Christianity included, some people distort, misuse, or abuse religion to incite violence and cause harm. We ought not allow these voices to determine or influence our perception of our neighbors. The ELCA must play an active role in dispelling fear of our neighbors, opposing religious bigotry, and standing with those who are the targets of fear, discrimination, hatred, and violence.

Inaction

Another possible response to religious diversity is inaction. For some of us, an encounter with religious difference may seem a distant reality or one we are not quite ready to acknowledge. We may have limited information and experiences, which can mean we are less motivated to reach out to our neighbors. All of us have been exposed to stereotypes, which may seem harmless when not acted on or spoken aloud. Yet, in the face of bigotry, such stereotypes are not neutral. They, too, can be destructive. Luther interprets the Eighth Commandment, "You shall not bear false witness against your neighbor," to mean not only that "we do not tell lies about our neighbors, betray or slander them, or destroy their reputations" but also that we should "come to their defense, speak well of them, and interpret everything they do in the best possible light" (Small Catechism). Such action is, in fact, required of us.

Active Engagement

When the alternatives are so devastating, respectful conversation, dialogue, advocacy, accompaniment, friendship, and cooperation are imperative. We are called to move beyond encountering our religiously diverse neighbors to actively engaging with them. This calling leads to concrete commitments that we strive to live out as people of faith. We are freed in Christ to engage our neighbors in a multi-religious world.

Expanding Our Inter-Religious Commitments

Our relationship to each of our neighbors of other religions and worldviews is vitally important. At the same time, Christians have had a particularly rich yet complex relationship with Jews and Muslims. In significantly different ways, all three traditions claim to worship the God of Abraham. Given this kinship, Lutherans have a responsibility to overcome stereotypes and misunderstandings of Muslims and Jews and to seek fuller understanding and cooperation. Doing so may well involve rethinking aspects of Christian self-understanding.

This "Declaration of Inter-Religious Commitment" reaffirms the 1994 "Declaration of the ELCA to the Jewish Community." At the same time, it extends the scope of our calling to additional neighbors too—including those of other religions, those who identify with multiple religious and spiritual traditions, and those who are not religious. Beyond Judaism and Islam, the ELCA engages with other religious communities, including Buddhists, Hindus, and Sikhs, among others. The state, national, and world councils of churches have played a significant role in expanding the breadth of our inter-religious dialogue and in exploring how we understand and relate to other neighbors who self-identify as Christian, but are not Trinitarian, such as the Church of Jesus Christ of Latter-day Saints and Jehovah's Witnesses. On the whole, we affirm the value of pursuing inter-religious dialogue in partnership with others whenever possible. The ELCA also participates in multi-religious coalitions, organizations, and initiatives that seek the common good. Though many religious traditions and worldviews are represented, these interactions provide opportunities for particular relationships to grow. As we are more frequently asked to articulate who we are and what we believe, multi-religious groups can also be spaces where we grow in our Lutheran self-understanding and vocation.

Occasions arise when reaching out directly as Lutherans is an important expression of our calling to love and serve our neighbor; for example, in response to an incident of religious bigotry or in pursuit of dialogue around a specific theological issue. Expanding and at the same time deepening our relations with our neighbors of other religions is a growing opportunity for the ELCA, and for the ecumenical movement as a whole. As our neighborhoods come to reflect greater religious diversity, our call to love and serve our neighbors also expands.

Relating to Neighbors Who Are Not Religious

This declaration focuses on neighbors who practice other religions. However, many people in the United States are religiously unaffiliated. Some, such as atheists or secular humanists, have rejected religion and a belief in God; others have affirmed individual spirituality over institutional and/or church affiliation. As Lutherans, we affirm that we are called to build relationships with all our neighbors. Many who are unaffiliated are longing to see Christians practicing the generosity and love they profess and are eager to cooperate on projects that improve the larger community. Such cooperation is a way of practicing our calling, as well as a way of giving authentic witness to our faith.

Pastoral Considerations

There are many pastoral considerations beyond the scope of this declaration, for example, the common reality of multi-religious family life. Therefore, the church recognizes the need for the ongoing development of appropriate pastoral aids, including guidelines for inter-religious marriages, pastoral counseling, religious education, and joint prayer services. In general, the ELCA is open to participating in inter-religious prayer services that honor the integrity, distinctive commitments, and gifts of each tradition, and reflect prayerful understanding and careful planning.

Vision

A biblical understanding of God's vision inspires our calling. The prophets received and shared this vision, and Jesus taught and embodied it.

A Biblical Vision

God's vision is of a world in which humans and creation, in all their glorious diversity, live in unity, justice, and peace. In such a world, hope abounds, and fear no longer separates one person from another or one people from another. In this vision, "justice roll[s] down like waters, and righteousness like an ever-flowing stream" (Amos 5:24) and "the leaves of the tree [of life] are for the healing of the nations" (Revelation 22:2b). We envision a world in which God's grace and mercy are celebrated, and all of God's creatures and all of God's creation are regarded with value and treated with care. The Scriptures reflect God's yearning for such a world, but they also recognize that we live between the inauguration of God's vision and its fulfillment. In the meantime, we struggle to "renounce the devil and all the forces that defy God" (*ELW*, Holy Baptism) as we experience the gift of Christ in us and the gift of the Holy Spirit calling us to celebrate every sign of reconciliation and wholeness.

As a community of faith, we are inspired to put God's vision into practice here and now, even if we can see only vague outlines of its fulfillment. We realize that we will fall short of the glory of God. Nevertheless, we live in love and hope. We seek to foster healthy relations and healthy communities in which all can flourish. We break the cycle of escalating retaliation that divides and destroys. With God's help, we seek to mend and heal the world that God so dearly and deeply loves.

Guided by God's vision and sobered by this realization, we seek, as one part of our undertaking, to achieve mutual understanding among all people of different religions and worldviews and to inspire all to work together for the common good. In doing so we give an account of the hope that is within us (1 Peter 3:15b).

Mutual Understanding

When we engage our religiously diverse neighbors, we can expect both a new understanding of the other and a deeper understanding and appreciation of our own Christian faith. "Mutual understanding" involves moving from factual knowledge of commonalities and differences to grasping coherence and even glimpsing beauty. In discovering how others love and cherish their religious traditions, we more deeply love and cherish our own. We empathize with the challenges and struggles others face in their religious commitments, as well as appreciate their joys. Mutual understanding opens the possibility of friendship and accepting responsibility for each other's well-being. As such, mutual understanding does not diminish but rather deepens our own faith.

Luther was clear that our understanding of faith can and does grow and change: as we experience new things in life, study and learn, and meditate and pray. Hence, a person's understanding can change without one's faith being undermined. By engaging our neighbors, we learn to articulate our own faith more clearly and to see in it things we had not noticed or appreciated before. We learn to express what being a follower of Jesus really means to us. We learn that religious differences need not erect barriers. In all of this, relying on the Holy Spirit, we experience more of the mystery and glory of God.

Common Good

As we strive to show forth God's vision, we are called to work toward justice and peace for all people and creation, that is, the common good. Religious diversity, when accompanied by mutual understanding and cooperation, enriches the whole. Through inter-religious relationships, we receive the gifts of our neighbors and experience more fully the exquisite realization that all are made in the image of God. A deep appreciation of the similarities and differences among religions and worldviews enhances working together for the common good. At the same time, cooperation can enhance both mutual understanding and the self-understanding of each participant. Seeking mutual understanding and the common good are active steps we can take toward God's vision of life abundant for all.

Calling

Our calling is a dual calling: to be faithful witnesses to Christ *and* to love God by loving and serving our neighbors. The Great Commission (Matthew 28:19–20) stands alongside the Great Commandment (Matthew 22:34–40).

Our Lutheran tradition distinguishes between "two kingdoms" of God. When Luther made this distinction, he was thinking not of two separate geographical territories but of two different ways, or "rules," in which God interacts with humans. These include: (1) showing mercy, overcoming our alienation, and giving us new life through Jesus Christ and (2) working through social, political, and economic institutions and authorities to safeguard human life and welfare.

Sharing the good news, or evangelism, contributes to the first rule. We do this in response to the Great Commission (Matthew 28:19–10). Serving the community, which includes inter-religious relations, contributes to the second. We do this in gratitude for God's mercy and in response to the Great Commandment to love God and to love our neighbor as ourselves (Matthew 22:39). In both rules, or kingdoms, God calls us to approach all relationships with love, grace, mercy, and a concern for distributive and restorative justice.

Evangelism

We are committed to engaging our neighbors without compromising who we are or the fullness of the calling we have received. An integral part of this calling is to be witnesses to Christ (Acts 1:8)—to evangelize. As understood by Lutherans, evangelism is sharing through our lives the joy of the good news of what God has done in and through Christ. This sharing occurs in many ways, in word and in deed—always respecting the dignity of the other and always offered in love. It occurs best in the context of an already established relationship of trust. We acknowledge that at times we have betrayed this trust, substituting manipulation and coercion for evangelism. As we express the power of life in Christ, we do so in ways that honor our convictions that every human is made in the image of God (Genesis 1:27) and that all of creation is good (Genesis 1:31).

We also rely on the Spirit, who alone creates faith. As we are taught in Luther's Small Catechism, "by my own understanding or strength I cannot believe in Jesus Christ my Lord or come to him, but instead the Holy Spirit has called me through the gospel [and] enlightened me with his gifts" (*ELW*, Explanation to the Third Article of the Apostles' Creed). We are saved by grace, unable to do anything to contribute to our own salvation, or to that of others.

Our faith compels us to respond to the gift we have received through the Spirit by freely and joyfully sharing the good news. We have claimed this evangelical commitment, and it is reflected even in our name. We know that "the Gospel is more than human recollection of, or our confession about, what God has done in the past. . . . It is proclamation with the power of God's deed in Christ and in his resurrection (2 Corinthians 5:19b–21), an event that opens to us the future of God's eternal love" ("A Declaration of Ecumenical Commitment," 1991).

With such a sure and certain promise, we anticipate that not only may God work through others, God may also work through us when we witness to a God of generosity and forgiveness, a God who loves humans, values their freedom, and works for their wholeness. As we engage our neighbors in the fullness of who we are and in whom we believe, we expect that so, too, will our partners share with us their deepest selves and convictions.

Inter-Religious Relations

Having received both the Great Commission and the Great Commandment, we recognize that inter-religious relations are part of our calling to love the neighbor. We are called by God and freed in Christ to witness to the life-changing news of Jesus Christ and to love and serve our neighbors in a multi-religious world. This vocation includes loving and serving both those who share our faith in Jesus Christ and those who do not. It is our duty and joy to extend God's love, grace, mercy, and justice to all those who are made in the image of God and to the whole of creation. In other words, we are called to inter-religious engagement because we are Lutheran. We live out this calling in three ways.

Love Our Neighbor

Central to the Lutheran tradition is every person's calling, or vocation, to love and serve God and our neighbor. As Luther reminded us, God asks that we direct our gratitude for God's generosity outward to others rather than upward in activities intended to please God. Luther called this our vocation. Alongside "grace alone," this was arguably his second most important teaching. Vocation affects every area of life. Our vocation, our calling to be a neighbor, excludes no one, even those whose religion is different from our own. Commenting on the parable of the Good Samaritan, Martin Luther defined the nei ghbor this way: "Now our neighbor is any human being, especially one who needs our help" (Martin Luther, "Letters to Galatians, 1535," *Luther's Works*). We are to extend God's mercy to all, and to love our neighbors as ourselves (Luke 10:25–37, Matthew 19:19).

Serve (Alongside) Our Neighbor

Our vocation includes service to the individual neighbor and to the community as a whole. To know how to best serve the community, we need to understand what benefits all parts of that community. This means reaching out to neighbors across the boundaries of religion, race, ethnicity, gender, and class. Our vocation also includes serving *alongside* our neighbor, as we respond together to meet the needs of others. While we may not necessarily share the same religious inspiration for doing so, our shared vision for peace and justice leads us to engage in service for the sake of the world.

Live in Solidarity with Our Neighbor

Being a neighbor can be risky. When power is abused, and fear grips a community or a nation, standing up for those who are being targeted or excluded takes courage. We are called to exhibit this courage and take this risk. In the face of social pressures that make us feel paralyzed, our calling includes developing a sense of agency—that is, a sense that each of us can make a difference. Our attention needs to be focused on our God-given gifts and responsibilities rather than on the many impediments to acting on behalf of those who are being maligned or harassed or harmed, recognizing that some of our neighbors are experiencing multiple forms of oppression at once. For all of this, a support community of fellow believers and inter-religious partners can make an empowering difference.

In the United States, many Christians live in neighborhoods that are predominantly Christian, where social expectations, such as holidays, school vacations, work rules, and the clothes we wear, have accommodated their beliefs and practices. The same is often not true for our neighbors who practice other religions or those who practice no religion at all. They can be at a disadvantage and made to feel like outsiders. As a result, we are called to be sensitive toward our neighbors of other religions and worldviews, engaging them in the spirit of accompaniment. This includes listening and learning, giving and receiving. It also means recognizing that other religions are organized differently, sometimes with very few or no structures corresponding to our own. Assumptions about cultural norms, affecting both ourselves and our neighbors, need to be constantly identified and avoided. Determining together the right pace for building and deepening partnerships is a way in which we can begin to practice mutual hospitality and live in solidarity with our neighbor. Our calling is to be both faithful witnesses and good neighbors. We enter into this calling in a spirit of humility and self-criticism, repentant of our past mistakes, anticipating that we will continue to fall short of God's vision, and committed to the justice, peace, and well-being of our neighbors. We accept that we will have unanswered questions about how God is working in and through our neighbors of other religions and even in and through us. Yet, we anticipate that in loving, serving, and standing in solidarity with our neighbors, we will experience the presence of God, participate in building a more just and peaceful world, and find our faith enriched.

Commitments

We participate in God's mission in an increasingly multi-religious world. Locally and globally, there are examples of religious communities coexisting peacefully but also examples of conflict, violence, discrimination, bigotry, intolerance, and persecution. In the midst of this, God has entrusted to us a vision of unity, justice, and peace. Therefore, in faithful response to God's love in Christ Jesus, we are called and committed to:

- Seek mutual understanding with our neighbors of other religions and worldviews.

- Cooperate with our neighbors of other religions and worldviews as instruments of God's justice and peace.

Across the ELCA, the form of our inter-religious relations will vary depending on context. As a church, we hold these commitments in common as a policy to guide our work and as a measure of accountability to our inter-religious partners.

1. The ELCA will pray for the well-being of our wonderfully diverse human family, including our neighbors of other religions and worldviews (*ELW*, Prayer for the Human Family, p. 79).
2. The ELCA will articulate why we both cherish the gospel, Scripture, the creeds, and confessions at the core of our Christian identity and Lutheran self-understanding and seek to understand our neighbor's core identity and self-understanding in a spirit of mutual respect ("Christian Witness in a Multi-Religious World: Recommendations for Conduct," the World Council of Churches, Pontifical Council for Interreligious Dialogue & World Evangelical Alliance, 2011).
3. The ELCA will witness to the power of life in Christ in and through our daily lives. We will seek to be ethical, transparent, and concerned for the integrity of our neighbor's rights and religious sensibilities as we share our faith with others (Report from Inter-Religious Consultation on Conversion, World Council of Churches, Pontifical Council for Interreligious Dialogue, 2006).
4. The ELCA, in dialogue with our partners, will seek to understand the religions of the world so as to enhance mutual understanding as well as to be able to identify the misuse of any religion to justify oppression, such as violence, genocide, or terrorism.
5. The ELCA will seek to know our neighbors in order to overcome stereotypes about them, "to come to their defense, speak well of them, and interpret everything they do in the best possible light" (Small Catechism, Eighth Commandment).
6. The ELCA will explore and encourage inter-religious friendship, accompaniment, and partnership with all who seek justice, peace, human wholeness, and the well-being of creation (ELCA Constitution, Chapter 4.03.f).
7. The ELCA will, whenever possible, work with other Christians and through ecumenical and inter-religious coalitions in its quest for inter-religious understanding and cooperation ("Lund Principle," 1952).
8. The ELCA will seek counsel from other religious groups in its discernment of and advocacy for the common good.

9. The ELCA will defend the full participation of all in our religiously diverse society, "strengthening public space as a just place for all" regardless of religion or worldview ("The Church in the Public Space: A Statement of The Lutheran World Federation," 2016).

10. The ELCA will defend human rights and oppose all forms of religious bigotry, violence, discrimination, and persecution and stand in solidarity with those who experience them, whether they are Christian or of another religion or worldview ("Human Rights" ELCA Social Message, 2017; "For Peace in God's World" ELCA Social Statement, 1995; "Freed in Christ: Race, Ethnicity, and Culture" ELCA Social Statement, 1993; "Church in Society: A Lutheran Perspective" ELCA Social Statement, 1991).

11. The ELCA will confess when our words or deeds (or lack thereof) cause offense, harm, or violence to our neighbors of other religions and worldviews and will repent and seek forgiveness from God and reconciliation with our neighbors ("Luther, Lutheranism, and Jews," The Lutheran World Federation, 1984; ELCA "Declaration to the Jewish Community," 1994; ELCA "Repudiation of the Doctrine of Discovery," 2016).

12. The ELCA will produce study and dialogue materials and pastoral guidelines for understanding and engaging with our neighbors of other religions and worldviews and seek counsel from inter-religious partners in the development of such resources.

Afterword: Biblical and Theological Underpinnings

As a policy statement, this document seeks to provide a common framework for inter-religious relations across the ELCA. This work takes a variety of forms and moves in differing directions. That is, dialogue can foster study, and study can lead to dialogue. Conversation can lead to cooperation, and cooperation can foster dialogue. Group experiences can produce one-to-one relationships, and one-to-one relationships can lead to group encounters. Whatever form inter-religious relations takes, the goal should be to achieve ever-deeper mutual understanding and to maximize cooperation for the sake of the world, and all of creation.

Many ELCA members and participants have experience with inter-religious relations. Their good work opens opportunities for us to replicate or to join rather than needing to invent or to initiate. It is not possible to provide a comprehensive list of these activities. Food banks, social service projects, and racial and economic justice work, when undertaken cooperatively with our neighbors of other religions and worldviews, are examples. So are advocacy endeavors, such as working for the care of creation or the reduction of HIV and AIDS. Some congregations share their buildings with other religious communities and find the relationship mutually enriching. ELCA colleges and seminaries have faculty, students, and courses that reflect religious diversity. They also have programs and groups that seek to foster sensitivity to religious difference and competencies for vocational living in a multi-religious world. When welcoming and receiving refugees as new neighbors, Lutherans have carefully and compassionately tended to the important dimensions of religion and culture. For more examples, see *Engaging Others, Knowing Ourselves: A Lutheran Calling in a Multi-Religious World* (Lutheran University Press, 2016).

While the framework offered by this policy statement is flexible, it is also firmly rooted in the scriptural, confessional, and theological witness of the Lutheran tradition. While we may undertake our calling to inter-religious relations in various contexts and ways, we do so undergirded by what we hold in common. Therefore, this declaration will close with an exploration of two key questions: "What do the Scriptures say about people of other religions?" and "What are some of the Lutheran convictions that influence our calling?"

What Do the Scriptures Say About People of Other Religions?
God's Vision

God's revelation has entrusted to us a vision of whole, healthy relationships among humans, between humans and the whole of creation, and between humans and God. Several passages in the Bible help us to see God's vision more clearly. We think of the wolf lying down with the lamb; swords beaten into plowshares and spears into pruning hooks; workers able to enjoy the fruits of the trees they have planted; people turning the other cheek and going the second mile; and a city with its gates wide open for all, with plenty of food, water, and medicine, and with God so close that no special building is needed (Isaiah 2:4, 65:21–22; Matthew 5:39–41; Revelation 21:22, 25 and 22:1–2). In light of God's vision, our calling is to help each other, and our neighbors, to make it manifest. With our lives, we become signs of this vision; through our whole, healthy relationships we come to see it more clearly. Our calling to live out this vision includes our relationships with our neighbors of other religions and worldviews. Every time we initiate, restore, heal, and embody such relationships, we take a step, however feebly, toward the wholeness that God intends. Our hope for the realization of God's vision guides and supports our calling and commitments.

Other Religions in the Bible

The Bible contains no uniform perspective regarding people of other religions. In some cases, the leaders of Israel try to draw a sharp line between the Israelites and their neighbors. In other cases, God is portrayed as working through neighbors who practice other religions. There are numerous examples:

- Moses receives valuable advice from Jethro, a priest of Midian, not an Israelite, who also happens to be his father-in-law (Exodus 18).

- Cyrus of Persia, who did not worship the God of Israel, is "anointed" by God to deliver the Israelites from exile (Isaiah 45:1).

- Jesus encounters a Canaanite woman and is moved by her faith to heal her daughter (Matthew 15:27).

- Jesus responds to the needs of a Roman centurion, a commander within the occupying forces—not likely a person who practiced Judaism (Matthew 8:5–13 and Luke 7:1–10).

- In the story of Abimelech, Abraham, and Sarah, it is the outsider Abimelech who listens to God and does what is right (Genesis 20).

- The Canaanite named Rahab hides the two spies Joshua sent to find out about Jericho prior to its conquest (Joshua 2).

- And the magi from the east, who likely did not practice Judaism, visit and honor the infant Jesus (Matthew 2:1–12).

These are but a few examples of how God loves and works with, in, and through people of various religions. These passages reveal the surprising truth that God at times invites Christians to learn from and even emulate people of other religions. These scriptural stories invite us to listen, ponder, and discover, from a position of humility, how God might use inter-religious relations to instruct us and challenge our faith to grow today.

What Lutheran Convictions Influence Our Calling?
Theology Is Relational

Lutheran theology is relational. Our religious communication needs to be assessed on whether it restores whole relationships and opens the door to new life or whether it harms another person or disregards the value of God's creation. When said in the wrong way or in the wrong setting, even "the right words" can be harmful. The same is true for actions. They, too, need to be evaluated in terms of their benefits or their damage to others and to the larger community. So, a relational theology examines both our words and actions in terms of whether they strengthen or undermine healthy relationships. This applies to words and actions that give expression to God's love and forgiveness (in response to the Great Commission) and to words and actions that seek to aid a struggling neighbor (in response to the Great Commandment).

Another indication of a theology that is relational is the Lutheran understanding of faith as trust. Faith is relational and not simply, or even primarily, about affirming beliefs. Faith is a response to the love of God, not a prerequisite for that love.

The observation that theology is relational helps us understand why Lutheran theology so often employs paradoxes—that is, it affirms as true two seemingly contradictory statements, such as "a Christian is a perfectly free lord of all, subject to none" and "a Christian is a perfectly dutiful servant of all, subject to all" (Luther, "The Freedom of a Christian"). Other examples are that God is both hidden and revealed and that a Christian is both justified and a sinner. This capacity for paradox can also be extended to the tension we hold between our dual commitments to evangelism and inter-religious relations. These formulations seek to point beyond themselves to a deeper truth that is relational rather than propositional. The stance of this declaration is influenced at every point by the relational character of Lutheran theology.

Grace Without Prerequisites

This declaration affirms and celebrates the gift of new life that comes from God but does not seek to explain God's relationship with other religions. There are several reasons for this. Our Lutheran tradition has emphasized that God's grace is given as a gift without any prerequisites. When God restores relations with us, it is entirely a result of God's action, not something we have earned. As a result, we cannot know the limits of God's grace and love. Any attempt to define a limit introduces a prerequisite. Because we do not know its limits, God's remarkable generosity toward us frees us to engage in inter-religious outreach, and in this way to embody for our neighbors God's generosity. Our calling is to come to know our neighbors, to assist them, to work with them, and in doing so to see in them the image of God.

Limits on Our Knowing

• The Lutheran tradition offers other reasons for caution about our claims to know.

• Luther said that no human could know another person's relationship with God. What that person says or does gives us clues, but, ultimately, we cannot see into someone else's heart (Luther, *Bondage of the Will*).

• Similarly, Luther insisted that we cannot know the inner workings of God. God has revealed God's attitude toward us, overall purpose, and character, but the inner workings of God remain hidden. Hence, we must be careful about claiming to know God's judgments regarding another religion or the individual human beings who practice it.

• There is another reason for caution. As mentioned above, the Lutheran tradition has understood the word "faith" to mean trust rather than affirming beliefs. Hence, we also must be careful not to judge our neighbors only on the basis of their religious beliefs, as they may or may not tell us much about how our neighbors relate to God. There is no substitute for exploring together what matters most to others and to us.

The full story of the relationship between our neighbor and God is beyond our knowledge, and even our calling. In the context of inter-religious relations, we do not need answers to these questions in order to treat one another with love and respect, find ways to cooperate for the sake of the larger community, practice hospitality, or witness to the good news of God's love, forgiveness, and new life in Christ. All we know, and all we need to know, is that our neighbors are made in God's image and that we are called to love and serve them.

Ever-Depending on Forgiveness

Our calling to inter-religious relations depends on God's forgiveness. We need to acknowledge not only our own personal errors and omissions but also the collective errors of our tradition. These include misdeeds, such as our readiness to benefit from the conquest of American Indian people and land, chattel slavery, the treatment of the Jews during and after the Reformation, and our readiness to take up arms against those of another religion. And they include failures to reach out to people of all races, ethnicities, and cultures within our church and in society. Not only do we rely on forgiveness for the past, we also rely on forgiveness for the present and the future.

Because our responsibility for others has no limits, inevitably our best efforts will fall short, and we are likely to make new mistakes that harm others. When we engage our neighbors, we therefore rely on forgiveness as we reach out into unfamiliar territory, navigating religious and cultural differences. The promise of forgiveness sets us free to risk the unfamiliar.

Acknowledging Suffering

At the heart of Luther's "theology of the cross" is a unique view of God present in the person of the crucified Jesus. Jesus' suffering on the cross was a redemptive suffering for the sake of all. The Jesus who endured the cross is also present with us, all humans, and the whole creation in times of suffering (Romans 8:18–25).

This understanding of a "theology of the cross" causes us to take the reality of suffering seriously. As Christian disciples we are called to take up the cross, acting on behalf of others to seek ways to end the suffering of others, even though doing so may lead us to suffer with them. This is part of our vocation as Christians. And, when ending suffering is not possible, we are still called to accompany—to be with—those who suffer, just as in Christ God came to be with us.

Acknowledging the reality of suffering unites us not only with God but also with one another. The commonality and universality of human suffering binds us inextricably to each other. This reality influences our understanding of our vocation. When we acknowledge the suffering of those whose beliefs are different from our own and when we recognize the commonality of suffering, we find a fuller, more compassionate understanding of those who differ and a common calling to alleviate suffering wherever it exists. At the same time, when we recognize the suffering of other Christians who experience discrimination or attacks because of their religious beliefs, we can appreciate how inter-religious relations can support not only cooperation but, indeed, survival. Amid suffering of all forms, we stand together, not apart.

God in the World

As we respond to our calling, we are confident that God is at work caring for all of creation, respecting human freedom and dignity, and fostering wholeness. We are sent out into the world by a God who is already at work. When we reach out to a neighbor, we are reaching out to someone who, whether the person acknowledges it or not, has already received gifts from God. In addition, just as the love of God reaches us through the words and actions of others, so our own words and actions can serve as "channels" (Luther's word) of God's gifts to others.

Conclusion and Benediction

We are called to learn to know and understand our neighbors and to work together for their well-being. We are called to work with them to overcome the obstacles and suffering they face, and to build justice and peace for all people and for God's creation. We are called to overcome the isolation that separates neighbors from one another. Having heard the good news of Jesus Christ, we are called to live in hope and engagement, not fear and inaction.

Our calling is a responsibility, yes, and it is also a joy. Engagement with our neighbors enriches our lives and our faith. In relationship with our neighbors, we come to understand more fully the depth and breadth of the riches of God and to appreciate more deeply the wonder of God's generous love, which we experience through the life, death, and resurrection of Jesus Christ. We discern more accurately how to reflect God's generosity in our thinking and in our behavior. As individuals and as neighbors, we benefit from the increased health of our communities and from a world that is more just and peaceful. Authentic and mutual relationships are transformative. May God bless the efforts of this church as we set our sights on God's vision, as we seek to respond to God's calling in our context, and as we strive to uphold these commitments.

Appendix 5:
Reclaiming Jesus
A Confession of Faith in a Time of Crisis[1]

We are living through perilous and polarizing times as a nation, with a dangerous crisis of moral and political leadership at the highest levels of our government and in our churches. **We believe the soul of the nation and the integrity of faith are now at stake.**

It is time to be followers of Jesus before anything else—nationality, political party, race, ethnicity, gender, geography—our identity in Christ precedes every other identity. We pray that our nation will see Jesus' words in us. "By this everyone will know that you are my disciples, if you have love for one another" (John 13:35).

When politics undermines our theology, we must examine that politics. The church's role is to change the world through the life and love of Jesus Christ. The government's role is to serve the common good by protecting justice and peace, rewarding good behavior while restraining bad behavior (Romans 13). When that role is undermined by political leadership, faith leaders must stand up and speak out. Rev. Dr. Martin Luther King Jr. said, "The church must be reminded that it is not the master or the servant of the state, but rather the conscience of the state."

It is often the duty of Christian leaders, especially elders, to speak the truth in love to our churches and to name and warn against temptations, racial and cultural captivities, false doctrines, and political idolatries—and even our complicity in them. We do so here with humility, prayer, and a deep dependency on the grace and Holy Spirit of God.

This letter comes from a retreat on Ash Wednesday, 2018. In this season of Lent, we feel deep lamentations for the state of our nation, and our own hearts are filled with confession for the sins we feel called to address. The true meaning of the word repentance is to turn around. It is time to lament, confess, repent, and turn. In times of crisis, the church has historically learned to return to Jesus Christ.

Jesus is Lord. That is our foundational confession. It was central for the early church and needs to again become central to us. If Jesus is Lord, then Caesar was not—nor any other political ruler since. If Jesus is Lord, no other authority is absolute. Jesus Christ, and the kingdom of God he announced, is the Christian's first loyalty, above all others. We pray, "Thy kingdom come, thy will be done, on earth as it is in heaven" (Matthew 6:10). Our faith is personal but never private, meant not only for heaven but for this earth.

The question we face is this: Who is Jesus Christ for us today? What does our loyalty to Christ, as disciples, require at this moment in our history? We believe it is time to renew our theology of public discipleship and witness. Applying what "Jesus is Lord" means today is the message we commend as elders to our churches.

What we believe leads us to what we must reject. Our "Yes" is the foundation for our "No." What we confess as our faith leads to what we confront. Therefore, we offer the following six affirmations of what we believe, and the resulting rejections of practices and policies by political leaders which dangerously corrode the soul of the nation and deeply threaten the public integrity of our faith. We pray that we, as followers of Jesus, will find the depth of faith to match the danger of our political crisis.

I. WE BELIEVE each human being is made in God's image and likeness (Genesis 1:26). That image and likeness confers a divinely decreed dignity, worth, and God-given equality to all of us as children of the one God who is the Creator of all things. Racial bigotry is a brutal denial of the image of God (the *imago dei*) in some of the children of God. Our participation in the global community of Christ absolutely prevents any toleration of racial bigotry. Racial justice and healing are biblical and theological issues for us, and are central to the mission of the body of Christ in the world. We give thanks for the prophetic role of the historic black churches in America when they have called for a more faithful gospel.

THEREFORE, WE REJECT the resurgence of white nationalism and racism in our nation on many fronts, including the highest levels of political leadership. We, as followers of Jesus, must clearly reject the use of racial bigotry for political gain that we have seen. In the face of such bigotry, silence is complicity. In particular, we reject white supremacy and commit ourselves to help dismantle the systems and structures that perpetuate white preference and advantage. Further, any doctrines or political strategies that use racist resentments, fears, or language must be named as public sin—one that goes back to the foundation of our nation and lingers on. Racial bigotry must be antithetical for those belonging to the body of Christ, because it denies the truth of the gospel we profess.

II. WE BELIEVE we are one body. In Christ, there is to be no oppression based on race, gender, identity, or class (Galatians 3:28). The body of Christ, where those great human divisions are to be overcome, is meant to be an example for the rest of society. When we fail to overcome these oppressive obstacles, and even perpetuate them, we have failed in our vocation to the world—to proclaim and live the reconciling gospel of Christ.

THEREFORE, WE REJECT misogyny, the mistreatment, violent abuse, sexual harassment, and assault of women that has been further revealed in our culture and politics, including our churches, and the oppression of any other child of God. We lament when such practices seem publicly ignored, and thus privately condoned, by those in high positions of leadership. We stand for the respect, protection, and affirmation of women in our families, communities, workplaces, politics, and churches. We support the courageous truth-telling voices of women, who have helped the nation recognize these abuses. We confess sexism as a sin, requiring our repentance and resistance.

III. WE BELIEVE how we treat the hungry, the thirsty, the naked, the stranger, the sick, and the prisoner is how we treat Christ himself. (Matthew 25: 31–46) "Truly I tell you, just as you did it to one of the least of these who are members of my family, you did it to me." God calls us to protect and seek justice for those who are poor and vulnerable, and our treatment of people who are "oppressed," "strangers," "outsiders," or otherwise considered "marginal" is a test of our relationship to God, who made us all equal in divine dignity and love. Our proclamation of the lordship of Jesus Christ is at stake in our solidarity with the most vulnerable. If our gospel is not "good news to the poor," it is not the gospel of Jesus Christ (Luke 4:18).

THEREFORE, WE REJECT the language and policies of political leaders who would debase and abandon the most vulnerable children of God. We strongly deplore the growing attacks on immigrants and refugees, who are being made into cultural and political targets, and we need to remind our churches that God makes the treatment of the "strangers" among us a test of faith (Leviticus 19:33–34). We won't accept the neglect of the well-being of low-income families and children, and we will resist repeated attempts to deny health care to those who most need it. We confess our growing national sin of putting the rich over the poor. We reject the immoral logic of cutting services and programs for the poor while cutting taxes for the rich. Budgets are moral documents. We commit ourselves to opposing and reversing those policies and finding solutions that reflect the wisdom of people from different political parties and philosophies to seek the common good. Protecting the poor is a central commitment of Christian discipleship, to which 2,000 verses in the Bible attest.

IV. WE BELIEVE that truth is morally central to our personal and public lives. Truth-telling is central to the prophetic biblical tradition, whose vocation includes speaking the Word of God into their societies and speaking the truth to power. A commitment to speaking truth, the ninth commandment of the Decalogue, "You shall not bear false witness" (Exodus 20:16), is foundational to shared trust in society. Falsehood can enslave us, but Jesus promises, "You will know the truth, and the truth will set you free." (John 8:32). The search and respect for truth is crucial to anyone who follows Christ.

THEREFORE, WE REJECT the practice and pattern of lying that is invading our political and civil life. Politicians, like the rest of us, are human, fallible, sinful, and mortal. But when public lying becomes so persistent that it deliberately tries to change facts for ideological, political, or personal gain, the public accountability to truth is undermined. The regular purveying of falsehoods and consistent lying by the nation's highest leaders can change the moral expectations within a culture, the accountability for a civil society, and even the behavior of families and children. The normalization of lying presents a profound moral danger to the fabric of society. In the face of lies that bring darkness, Jesus is our truth and our light.

V. WE BELIEVE that Christ's way of leadership is servanthood, not domination. Jesus said, "You know that the rulers of the Gentiles (the world) lord it over them, and their great ones are tyrants over them. It will not be so among you; but whoever wishes to be great among you must be your servant" (Matthew 20:25–26). We believe our elected officials are called to public service, not public tyranny, so we must protect the limits, checks, and balances of democracy and encourage humility and civility on the part of elected officials. We support democracy, not because we believe in human perfection, but because we do not. The authority of government is instituted by God to order an unredeemed society for the sake of justice and peace, but ultimate authority belongs only to God.

THEREFORE, WE REJECT any moves toward autocratic political leadership and authoritarian rule. We believe authoritarian political leadership is a theological danger that threatens democracy and the common good—and we will resist it. Disrespect for the rule of law, not recognizing the equal importance of our three branches of government and replacing civility with dehumanizing hostility toward opponents are of great concern to us. Neglecting the ethic of public service and accountability, in favor of personal recognition and gain often characterized by offensive arrogance, are not just political issues for us. They raise deeper concerns about political idolatry, accompanied by false and unconstitutional notions of authority.

VI. WE BELIEVE Jesus when he tells us to go into all nations making disciples (Matthew 28:18). Our churches and our nations are part of an international community whose interests always surpass national boundaries. The most well-known verse in the New Testament starts with "For God so loved the world" (John 3:16). We, in turn, should love and serve the world and all its inhabitants, rather than seek first narrow, nationalistic prerogatives.

THEREFORE, WE REJECT "America first" as a theological heresy for followers of Christ. While we share a patriotic love for our country, we reject xenophobic or ethnic nationalism that places one nation over others as a political goal. We reject domination rather than stewardship of the earth's resources, toward genuine global development that brings human flourishing for all of God's children. Serving our own communities is essential, but the global connections between us are undeniable. Global poverty, environmental damage, violent conflict, weapons of mass destruction, and deadly diseases in some places ultimately affect all places, and we need wise political leadership to deal with each of these.

WE ARE DEEPLY CONCERNED for the soul of our nation, but also for our churches and the integrity of our faith. The present crisis calls us to go deeper—deeper into our relationship to God; deeper into our relationships with each other, especially across racial, ethnic, and national lines; deeper into our relationships with the most vulnerable, who are at greatest risk.

The church is always subject to temptations to power, to cultural conformity, and to racial, class, and gender divides, as Galatians 3:28 teaches us. But our answer is to be "in Christ," and to "not be conformed to this world, but be transformed by the renewing of your minds, so that you may discern what is the will of God—what is good and acceptable, and perfect." (Romans 12:1–2)

The best response to our political, material, cultural, racial, or national idolatries is the First Commandment: "You shall have no other gods before me" (Exodus 20:3). Jesus summarizes the Greatest Commandment: "You shall love the Lord your God with all your heart, your soul, and your mind. This is the first commandment. And the second is like unto it. You shall love your neighbor as yourself. On these commandments hang all the law and the prophets" (Matthew 22:38). As to loving our neighbors, we would add "no exceptions."

We commend this letter to pastors, local churches, and young people who are watching and waiting to see what the churches will say and do at such a time as this. Our urgent need, in a time of moral and political crisis, is to recover the power of confessing our faith. Lament, repent, and then repair. If Jesus is Lord, there is always space for grace. We believe it is time to speak and to act in faith and conscience, not because of politics, but because we are disciples of Jesus Christ—to whom be all authority, honor, and glory. It is time for a fresh confession of faith. Jesus is Lord. He is the light in our darkness. "I am the light of the world. Whoever follows me will not walk in darkness but will have the light of life" (John 8:12).[1]

Acknowledgments

We are grateful to a number of people and organizations who made this publication possible. First, our thanks to Brad Lyons, president and publisher of Chalice Press, for his faith in this project. Second, we want to express our gratitude to Rev. Peter Marty, publisher of *The Christian Century Magazine*, for writing the Foreword, and also to Rev. Dr. Herbert E. Anderson for providing the Preface and other resources.

Below are listed others with whom we consulted during the course of the writing project, who gave generously of their time and resources, some of whom appear in the appendices:

Rev. Lyle McKenzie and Rev. Paul Gehrs, assistants to the National Bishop, Evangelical Lutheran Church in Canada. They provided invaluable information related to the "Truth and Reconciliation" process with First Nations People in Canada. A Liturgy of Repentance and Reconciliation written by Rev. Sean Bell and Rev. Stewart Miller, ELCIC pastors, in collaboration with the First Nation people of Canada is reprinted by permission.

Ms. Collen Geyer, general secretary of the Uniting Church of Australia and the Rev. Ian Price, UCA. *The Day of Mourning* Worship Resource prepared by the UCA in collaboration with United Aboriginal and Islander Christian Conference is reprinted by permission.

Rev. Elizabeth Eaton, presiding Bishop; Sue Rothmeyer, secretary; and Rev. Wm. Chris Boerger, retired secretary, of the Evangelical Lutheran Church in America. Two ELCA churchwide documents on social issues are reprinted by permission.

Rev. Terry Kyllo, Rev. Diakonda Gurning, and retired Bishop Kirby Unti provided important information regarding interfaith relationships in Washington State.

Rev. Dr. Ray Pickett, Rector of Pacific Lutheran Theological Seminary and Biblical scholar whose teaching offered insights into the radical nature of the Gospel narrative.

The Northwest African American Museum in Seattle and its executive director LaNesha DeBardelaben, for helping us better understand the African American experience.

The Holocaust Museum and Learning Center (St. Louis, MO) and the Dayton International Peace Museum (Dayton, OH) for making available valuable resources.

Imam Jamal Rahman, Interfaith Community Sanctuary (Seattle, WA) and Rabbi Rachel Kort, Temple Beth Or (Everett, WA) who offered encouragement and support.

Beth Lewis, president and CEO emeritus of 1517 Media, who spend countless hours editing our manuscript.

The Seattle Council of Churches and Lutheran Immigration and Refugee Services. Their ecumenical work among the indigenous people of Washington and among new immigrants—representing many ethnic groups and religious traditions—is to be commended.

Notes

Preface

1. Herbert Anderson, "Seeing the Other Whole: A Habitus for Globalization," in *Mission Studies*, vol. xiv, 1 & 2, no. 27 & 28, fall, 1997, 1. (Reprinted in *Globalization and Difference: Practical Theology in World Context*, edited by Paul Ballard and Pam Courture. Cardiff, England: Cardiff Academic Press, 1999.)

"Canticle of the Turning" by Rory Cooney

1. Chicago: GIA Publications, Inc. ©1990. Used with permission.

Chapter 1

1. Clyde W. Ford, "Servants or slaves? How Africans First Came to America Matters," *Seattle Times*, August 20, 2019, A11.

2. Billy Graham: "America is Not God's Only Kingdom" by Marguerite Michaels, p. 17 *Parade Magazine*, February 1, 1981.

3. Mark Labberton, "Political Dealing: The Crisis of Evangelicalism," *Fuller News Online*, April 20, 2018.

4. For more information check the following link, https://www.pewtrusts.org/en/topics/religion.

5. Kenneth Inskeep, Report to Covenant Cluster of the Evangelical Lutheran Church in America, Feb. 20–22, 2014.

6. Linda Mercadante, *Belief Without Borders: Inside the Minds of the Spiritual but Not Religious* (New York: Oxford University Press, 2014), 1.

7. Stephen Mattson, "Have We Forgotten the Point of Christianity?" *Sojourners*, Oct. 13, 2016. Accessed at www.Sojo.net.

8. Marcus Borg, *Jesus: Uncovering the Life, Teachings, and Relevance of a Religious Revolutionary* (New York: Harper Collins, 2015), 20.

9. E. J. Dionne, Jr., "Reclaiming Jesus." *Washington Post Online*, May 23, 2017.

10. Walter Brueggemann, *A Way Other Than Our Own* (Louisville: Westminster John Knox Press, 2017), 4.

11. "Let America Be America Again" from *The Collected Poems of Langston Hughes* by Langston Hughes, edited by Arnold Rampersad with David Roessel, Associate Editor, copyright ©1994 by the Estate of Langston Hughes. Used by permission of Alfred A. Knopf, an imprint of the Knopf Doubleday Publishing Group, a division of Penguin Random House LLC. All rights reserved. Check out the following link for the complete poem: https://poets.org/poem/let-america-be-america-again

Chapter 2

1. Kristin Hannah, *The Nightingale* (New York: St. Martins Press, 2015), 410.

2. Ryan W. Miller, "Whites Worry About Minorities in Majority," *USA Today*, March 22, 2019, 3A.

3. Miller, Ibid.

4. Herbert Anderson, "Seeing the Other Whole: A Habitus for Globalization," in *Mission Studies*, vol. xiv, 1 & 2, no. 27 & 28, fall, 1997, 4. (Reprinted in *Globalization and Difference: Practical Theology in World Context*, edited by Paul Ballard and Pam Couture. Cardiff, England: Cardiff Academic Press, 1999.)

5. William H. Willimon, *Fear of the Other: No Fear in Love* (Nashville: Abingdon Press, 2016), 7.

6. James H. Cone, *The Cross and the Lynching Tree* (Maryknoll, NY: Orbis, 2011), xiv–xv.

7. "Easter Evil," *The Economist,* April 27, 2019, 12.

8. Bryan A. Garner, ed. *Black's Law Dictionary* (Eagan, MN: Thomson West), 2019.

9. Paul Louis Metzger, "What Is Biblical Justice?" *Christianity Today*, Summer 2010: 17.

10. Richard Rohr, *Another Way to See Justice: An Intro Email Series with Richard Rohr* Center for Action and Contemplation. June 1, 2019. For more information, check out the following link: meditations@cac.org.

11. "Dialogues on the Refugee Crisis," DVD Session One (Minneapolis: Spark House), 2019.

12. Walter Bruggemann, Ibid., 20–21.

13. Renate Wind, "A Spoke in the Wheel: Dietrich Bonhoeffer and His Development into Political Resistance," Lecture at Pacific Lutheran University, Tacoma, WA (August 28, 2018), 4–5.

14. Wind, Ibid., 6.

15. Mark Brocker, "For the Love of the World: Bonhoeffer's Resistance to Hitler and the Nazis," Lecture at Pacific Lutheran University, Tacoma, WA (August 28, 2018), 10.

16. Brocker, Ibid., 17–18.

17. Brocker, Ibid., 20.

18. From the National Nordic Museum, Seattle, Washington.

19. William Whitla, "Let Streams of Living Justice" © 1989. Used by permission of the author.

Chapter 3

1. See Daniel 7:13–14.

2. See Micah 6:8.

3. Willimon, op cit., 89–90.

4. Archbishop Dmitri, *The Parables: Biblical, Patristic and Liturgical Interpretation* (Crestwood New York: St. Vladimir's Seminary Press, 1996), 118.

5. Unfortunately, Luther was not so charitable toward the Jewish population, reflecting the prejudice of his day.

6. Nick Miroff, "Border Officials Spent Emergency Humanitarian Funds on Dirt Bikes, Dogs, and Enforcement Programs According to Government Reports." *Washington Post Online*, June 11, 2020.

7. Peter Marty, *The Christian Century*, May 9, 2018, 3.

8. Sign posted in the narthex of Holy Spirit Lutheran Church, Kirkland, Washington.

9. Shelly Bryan Wee, "Regarding Sanctuary," Northwest Washington Synod, ELCA, August 13, 2019.

10. Julie Watson and Elliot Spagat, *The Seattle Times*, May 10, 2019, A5.

11. Bishop Michael Curry, from his wedding sermon to Prince Harry and Meghan Markle, at St. George's Chapel at Windsor Castle, May 19, 2018.

Chapter 4

1. From the documentary film *Emanuel*, directed by Brian Ivie, 2019.

2. Miranda Green, Derek Hawkins, and Scott Wilson, "Nooses Hangings and Cross Burnings: Imagery of America's Dark Racial History Sparks Fear Nationwide." *Washington Post Online*, June 24, 2020.

3. Jason Easley, "Trump Goes Full Racist and Accuses Black Lives Matter of Treason." *Politicus USA*, June 25, 2020. For full article check out the following link: www.politicususa.com/2020/06/25/trump-black-lives-matter-treason.html

4. Excerpt from the 2019 play "Small Island" by playwright Helen Edmundson based on the 2004 novel by the same name by Andrea Levy.

5. For the full text of the Public Declaration check out the following link: https://thechurchcouncil.org/wp-content/uploads/2016/09/1987_Apology_to_the _tribes_of_the_NorthWest.pdf.

6. *Declaration of Evangelical Lutheran Church in America to the Jewish Community*, April 18, 1994.

7. Elizabeth Eaton, "ELCA Presiding Bishop Issues Pastoral Message on Racism and White Supremacy," *ELCA News*, September 13, 2019.

8. Desmond Tutu, *The Book of Forgiving: The Four-Fold Path for Healing Ourselves and Our World* (San Francisco: Harper One, 2015).

9. From the 1948 Definition of Genocide by the United Nations. See the following link: https://www.un.org/ar/preventgenocide/adviser/pdf/osapg_analysis _framework.pdf.

10. For reconciliation resources from the Anglican Church of Canada check out the following link: https://www.anglican.ca/resources-category/truth-reconciliation.

11. For more information about Canada's Truth and Reconciliation Commission check out the following link: https://www.rcaanc-cirmac.gc.ca.

12. Quote and information from an article by Gustavo Arellano, *The Seattle Times*, February 17, 2020; A6.

13. Stephen J. Patterson, *The Forgotten Creed: Christianity's Original Struggle against Bigotry, Slavery, and Sexism.* (New York: Oxford University Press, 2018), 22.

14. David Haas, "We Are Called," Chicago: GIA Publications, Inc. ©1988. Used with permission.

Chapter 5

1. For more information about the *Peace Labyrinth: Quilting the Golden Rule*, check out the following website: https://daytonpeacemuseum.org/.

2. Verse 8 is author Paul Ingram's translation.

3. For a definition see: https://reformjudaism.org/tanach-0.

4. In Greek, *basileia tou theou*, translated as "kingdom of God" in the New Testament, but a more accurate translation is "commonwealth of God."

5. Genesis 32:24–31. Also see Paul O. Ingram, *Wrestling with God* (Eugene, OR: Cascade Books, 2006).

6. See Paul O. Ingram, *Living Without a Why* (Eugene, OR: Cascade Books, 2014), Chapter 7.

7. Luke 16:13 = Matt 6:24; Luke 6:44 = Matt 7:16; Luke 8: 16–17 = Matt 5:14; Luke 9:60 = Matt 8:22; Matt 23:4.

8. See Luke 10:25–37.

9. *Diwan-i-Shams-i-Tabrizi, i*, ("*The Works of Shams of Tabriz*"), cited in Annemarie Schimmel, *The Mystical Dimensions of Islam* (Chapel Hill, NC: University of North Carolina Press, 1975), 134.

10. W. J. Astin (trans), *The Bezels of Wisdom,* by Idn al Arabi. Classics of Western Spirituality. (New York: Paulist Press, 1981), 103.

11. In the Theravada Buddhist Way rooted in South Asia, the monastic community; in the Mahayana Buddhist Way that originated in East Asia. The entire community of Buddhists, both monks, nuns, and laity—although primary emphasis is still given to cloistered communities of monks and nuns.

12. Sally B. King, "Thich Nhất Hahn and the United Buddhist Church of Vietnam: Nondualism in Action," in *Engaged Buddhism: Buddhist Liberation Movements in Asia.* Edited by Christopher S. Queen and Sallie B. King (Albany: State University of New York, 1996), 402–456.

13. Sallie B. King, "Through the Eyes of Auschwitz and the Killing Fields: Mutual Learning between Engaged Buddhism and the Killing Fields" lecture presented at the Annual Meeting of the Society for Buddhist-Christian Studies, San Diego, CA (November 24, 2014).

14. Translated by Arthur Waley in *The Way and Its Power: A Study of the Tao De Ching and Its Place in Chinese History* (New York: Grove Press, 1958), 238.

Chapter 6

1. Attributed to Spread Kindness.

2. In Christ There Is No East or West," text by John Oxenham. Evangelical Lutheran Worship (Minneapolis: Augsburg Fortress Publishers, 2006).

3. Richard Rohr. *The Universal Christ: How a Forgotten Reality Can Change Everything We See, Hope For, and Believe* (New York: Convergent Books, 2019), 47–48.

4. See Van Harvey, *The Historian and the Believer* (Philadelphia: Westminster Press, 1966), chapters 3–8.

5. *Augsburg Confession*, Article 29, 16–26.

Chapter 7

1. President John F. Kennedy, Civil Rights Speech, June 11, 1963. For full transcript check the following link: https://highered.nbclearn.com/portal/site/HigherEd/flatview?cuecard=1679.

2. Modified from material by Herbert Anderson and Robert Schreiter. Used with permission.

3. *Constitution of the Evangelical Lutheran Church in America* (ELCA Churchwide: Chicago, IL, 1988).

4. Reported by Vivienne Walt, "The Hatred Stalking Europe" (*Time*, July 1, 2019), 39–42.

5. Adapted from Marcus Harrison Green, "Peace Camp Plans Seeds for Change in Middle East and in Seattle," *Seattle Times*, July 16, 2019, B1–B5.

6. Adapted from a lecture by Angel Swanson, "How to Talk to Your Racist Uncle," March 16, 2019.

7. Adapted from the Developmental Model of Intercultural Sensitivity by Milton Bennett. See the following link: https://www.idrinstitute.org/dmis/.

8. Eric Law, Guidelines for Respectful Communication. From his book *Inclusion: Making Room for Grace* (St. Louis: Chalice Press, 2000), 64.

9. Carol Schersten LaHurd, ed., *Engaging Others, Knowing Ourselves: A Lutheran Calling in a Multi-Religious World* (Minneapolis: Lutheran University Press, 2016), 65.

10. *Madam Secretary*, CBS, October 8, 2018.

11. Poem by Emma Lazarus, Inscribed on the Statue of Liberty, New York Harbor.

12. "Progression of Hate Diagram" used with permission of the St. Louis Jewish Community Archives and Holocaust Museum, St. Louis, MO.

13. Gregory H. Stanton. "The Ten Stages of Genocide," a paper published by Genocide Watch: Washington, DC, 2013. For full text, see http://www.genocide watch.org/genocide/tenstagesofgenocide.html.

14. Richard Dawahare, "Honoring My Uncle: An American Success Story Forged in Love and Civility" (Lexington, Kentucky: *Lexington Herald Leader*), July 25, 2019.

15. Senator Edward Kennedy, eulogy for Robert Kennedy, June 8, 1968. For full transcript check following link: https://www.washingtonpost.com/news/retropolis /wp/2018/06/08/those-he-touched-ted-kennedys-heartbreaking-eulogy-for-his -slain-brother-bobby/?noredirect=on&utm_term=.b6274f961fd3.

Epilogue

1. Ron Dreher, *The Benedict Option: A Strategy for Christians in a Post-Christian Nation* (New York: Penguin Random House, 2017), 16.

2. George W. Bush, video clip on Facebook, May 1, 2020.

3. *Seattle Times*, April 11, 2020, p. A4.

4. William Saletan, "Trump is Losing His Grip on White America." *Slatest Newsletter*, June 20, 2020, p. 3.

5. Ibid., May 4, 2020, p. A14.

6. Ibid., April 6, 2020, p. A16.

Appendix 1

1. *Day of Mourning.* The Uniting Church in Australia, 2018.

2. *Bäpa means father in the Yolŋu languages of NE Arnhemland and in Bahasa languages*

Appendix 2

1. *Liturgy of Repentance and Reconciliation.* The Evangelical Lutheran Church in Canada. 2019. Used with permission.

Appendix 3

1. *Declaration of the ELCA to People of African Descent.* Adopted by the 2019 ELCA Churchwide Assembly. Used with permission.

2. *Freed in Christ: Race, Ethnicity, and Culture* (Chicago: Evangelical Lutheran Church in America, 1993), 4-5.

3. *The Church and Criminal Justice: Hearing the Cries* (Chicago: Evangelical Lutheran Church in America, 2013).

4. *Freed in Christ: Race, Ethnicity, and Culture* (Chicago: Evangelical Lutheran Church in America, 1993), 2. https://www.elca.org/Faith/Faith-and-Society/Social- Statements/Race-Ethnicity-and-Culture.

5. Robert P. Forbes, *"Notes on the State of Virginia* (1785)," Encyclopedia Virginia, paragraph 17. www.encyclopediavirginia.org/ Notes_on_the_State_of_Virginia_1785.

6. US Const, Amend XIII. https://www.law.cornell.edu/constitution /amendmentxiii

7. Michelle Alexander, *The New Jim Crow: Mass Incarceration in the Age of Colorblindness* (New York: The New Press, 2012), 13. 5 *The Church and Criminal*

Justice: Hearing the Cries (Chicago: Evangelical Lutheran Church in America, 2013), 14.

8. *The Church and Criminal Justice: Hearing the Cries* (Chicago: Evangelical Lutheran Church in America, 2013), 14.

9. Equal Justice Initiative, *Lynching in America: Confronting the Legacy of Racial Terror*, 3rd Ed. (2017), paragraph 9. https://lynchinginamerica.eji.org/report/.

10. *Freed in Christ*, 6.

11. "Troubling the Waters for Healing of the Church: A Journey for White Christians From Privilege to Partnership" (Chicago: Evangelical Lutheran Church in America, 2004).

12. R.M. Chapman, "Just Enough? Lutherans, Slavery, and the Struggle for Racial Justice," *The Cresset (LXXI)* 5 (2008), 16-20. http://thecresset.org/2008/Trinity2008/Chapman_T2008.html.

13. Ibid., paragraph 10.

14. L. Vox, "3 Major Ways Slaves Showed Resistance to Slavery," Thoughtco (retrieved July 2, 2019). https://www.thoughtco.com/ways-slaves-showed-resistance-to-slavery-45401.

15. Frederick Douglass, "West India Emancipation," *University of Rochester Frederick Douglass Project: Writings* (Rochester, NY: University of Rochester, 1998-2018), paragraphs 31, 43. https://rbscp.lib.rochester.edu/4398.

Appendix 4

1. *A Declaration of Our Inter-Religious Commitment: A Policy Statement of the Evangelical Lutheran Church in America.* Adopted by the 2019 ELCA Churchwide Assembly. Used with permission.

Appendix 5

1. *Reclaiming Jesus: A Confession of Faith in a Time of Crisis.* "Reclaiming Jesus Elders"(www.reclaimingjesus.org.) Used with permission.

Bibliography

Barndt, Joseph. *Becoming an Anti-Racist Church: Journeying Toward Wholeness*. Minneapolis: Fortress Press, 2011.

Beck, Richard. *Stranger God: Meeting Jesus in Disguise*. Minneapolis, MN: Fortress Press, 2017.

Birkel, Michael. *Qur'an in Conversation*. Waco, TX: Baylor University Press, 2014.

Bonhoeffer, Dietrich. *Life Together*. Minneapolis, MN: Fortress Press, 2015.

Brueggemann, Walter. *A Way Other Than Our Own*. Louisville, KY: Westminster John Knox Press. 2017.

Chittister, Joan. *The Time Is Now: A Call to Uncommon Courage*. New York: Crown Publishing Group, 2019.

Coffman, Kristofer, and et al. *Dialogues on Race*. Minneapolis, MN: Spark House, 2019.

Cone, James. *The Cross and the Lynching Tree*. Maryknoll, NY: Orbis, 2011.

Dark, David. *The Possibility of America: How the Gospel Can Mend Our God-Blessed, God- Forsaken Land*. Louisville, KY: Westminster John Knox Press, 2019.

Daughrity, Dryon B. *Rising: The Amazing Story of Christianity's Resurrection in the Global South*. Minneapolis, MN: Fortress Press, 2018.

deGruchy, John. *The End Is Not Yet: Standing Firm in Apocalyptic Times*. Minneapolis, MN: Fortress Press, 2017.

DeWolf, Thomas Norman and Sharon Morgan. *Gather at the Table: The Healing Journey of a Daughter of Slavery and a Son of the Slave Trade*. Boston, MA: Beacon Press, 2012.

DiAngelo, Robin. *White Fragility: Why It's So Hard for White People to Talk About Racism*. Boston, MA: Beacon Press, 2018.

Dreher, Rod. *The Benedict Option: A Strategy for Christians in a Post-Christian Nation*. New York: Sentinel, 2017.

Duckworth, Jessicah. *Wide Welcome: How the Unsettling Presence of Newcomers Can Save the Church*. Minneapolis, MN: Augsburg Fortress, 2013.

Duncan, Lenny. *Dear Church: A Love Letter from a Black Preacher to the Whitest Denomination in the U.S.* Minneapolis, MN: Fortress Press, 2019.

Ellingsen, Mark. *When Did Jesus Become a Republican? Rescuing Our Country and Our Values from the Right*. Lanham, MD: Rowman & Littlefield Publishers, 2007.

Farlee, Robert Buckley and Beth Ann Gaede, Editors. *Honoring Our Neighbor's Faith*. Minneapolis, MN: Augsburg Fortress, 2016.

Fox, Matthew. *One River, Many Wells: Wisdom Springing from Global Faiths*. New York: Jeremy P. Tarcher/Putnam, 2000.

Fredricksen, Paula. *When Christians Were Jews: The First Generation.* New Haven, CT: Yale University Press, 2018.

Granberg-Michaelson, Wesley. *Future Faith: Ten Challenges Reshaing Christianity in the 21st Century.* Minneapolis, MN: Fortress Press, 2018.

Green, Todd. *The Fear of Islam: An Introduction to Islamaphobia in the West.* Minneapolis, MN: Fortress Press, 2019.

Gushee, David. *Still Christian: Following Jesus out of American Evangelicalism.* Louisville, KY: Westminster John Knox Press, 2017.

Hilton, Allen. *A House United: How the Church Can Save the World.* Minneapolis, MN: Fortress Press, 2018.

Ingram, Paul. *You Have Been Told What Is Good: Interreligious Dialogue and Climate Change.* Eugene, OR: Cascade Books, 2016.

Jenkins, Jack. *American Prophets: The Religious Roots of Progressive Politics and the* Ongoing *Fight for the Soul of the Country.* New York: Harper Collins, 2020.

Jones, Robert P. *White Too Long: The Legacy of White Supremacy in American   Christianity.* New York: Simon and Schuster, 2020.

Law, Eric. *Inclusion: Making Room for Grace.* St. Louis, MO: Chalice Press, 2000.

Law, Eric. *The Word at the Crossings: Living the Good News in a Multi-Contexual Community.* St. Louis, MO: Chalice Press, 2004.

LaHurd, Carol Schersten, Editor. *Engaging Others, Knowing Ourselves: A Lutheran Calling in a Multi-Religious World.* Minneapolis, MN: Lutheran University Press, 2016.

MacKenzie, Don, Ted Falcon, and Jamal Rahman. *Religon Gone Astray: What We Found at the Heart of Interfaith.* Woodstock, VT: Skylight Paths Publishing, 2015.

Mahu, Jason. *Becoming a Christian in Christendom: Radical Discipleship and the Way of the Cross in America's "Christian" Culture.* Minneapolis: Fortress Press, 2016.

McLaren, Brian. *The Great Spiritual Migration: How the World's Largest Religoin Is Seeking a Better Way to Be Christian.* New York: Convergent Books, 2016.

McLaren, Brian. *Why Did Jesus, Moses, the Buddha, and Mohammed Cross the Road? Christian Identity in a Multifaith World.* New York: Jericho Books, 2012.

Mecklenburger, Ralph D. *Our Religious Brains: What Cognitive Science Reveals about Belief, Morality, Community, and Our Relationship with God.* Woodstock, VT: Jewish Lights Publishing and Skylight Paths Publishing, 2012.

Murphy, Timothy Charles. *Sustaining Hope in an Unjust World: How to Keep Going When You Want to Give Up.* St. Louis, MO: Chalice Press, 2019.

Nikondeha, Kelley. *Adopted: The Sacrament of Belonging in a Fractured World.* Grand Rapids, MI: Wm. B. Eerdmans Publishing, 2017.

Patterson, Stephen J. *The Forgotten Creed: Christianity's Original Struggle against Bigtry, Slavery, and Sexism.* New York: Oxford University Press, 2018.

Pohl, Christine. *Making Room: Recovering Hospitality as a Christian Tradition.* Grand Rapids, MI: Wm. B. Eerdmans Publishing, 1999.

Rogers, Melissa. *Faith in American Public Life.* Waco, TX: Baylor, 2019.

Rohr, Richard. *The Universal Christ: How a Forgotten Reality Can Change Everything We See, Hope For, and Believe.* New York: Convergent, 2019.

Rouse, Rick. *Beyond Church Walls: Cultivating a Culture of Care.* Minneapolis, MN: Fortress Press, 2016.

Rouse, Rick. *Fire of Grace: The Healing Power of Forgiveness.* Minneapolis: Augsburg Books, 2005.

Russell, Letty. *Just Hospitality: God's Welcome in a World of Difference.* Louisville, KY: Westminster John Knox Press, 2009.

Stevenson, Brian. *Just Mercy: A Story of Justice and Redemption.* New York: Spiegel and Grau, 2014.

Tietz, Christiane. *Theologian of Resistance: The Life and Thought of Dietrich Bonhoeffer.* Minneapolis, MN: Fortress Press, 2016.

Turner, Dale. *Another Way: Open-Minded Faithfulness.* Homewood, IL: High Tide Press, 2000.

Van Engen, Lisa. *And Social Justice for All: Empowering Families, Churches, and Schools to Make a Difference in God's World.* Grand Rapids, MI: Kregel, 2019.

Vanhoozer, Kevin, and Owne Strachan. *The Pastor as Public Theologian: Reclaiming a Lost Vision.* Grand Rapids, MI: Baker Academic, 2015.

Volf, Miroslav. *Exclusion and Embrace.* Nashville, TN: Abingdon, 2019.

Wallis, Jim. *America's Original Sin: White Privilege and the Bridge to a New America.* Ada, MI: Baker Books, 2016.

Wallis, Jim. *God's Politics: Why the Right Gets It Wrong and the Left Doesn't Get It.* New York: HarperCollins Publishers, 2005.

Wallis, Jim. *What about Jesus? Finding a Place to Stand in a Time of Crisis.* New York: Harper One, 2019.

Waldman, Steve. *Sacred Liberty: America's Long, Bloody, and Ongoing Struggle for Religious Freedom.* New York: Harper One, 2019.

Wee, Paul. *American Destiny and the Calling of the Church.* Minneapolis, MN: Augsburg Fortress, 2006.

White, Rozella Haydee. *Love Big: The Power of Revolutionary Relationships to Heal the World.* Minneapolis, MN: Fortress Press, 2019.

Williamson, Marianne. *A Politics of Love: A Handbook for a New American Revolution.* New York: Harper One, 2019.

Willimon, William. *Fear of the Other: No Fear in Love.* Nashville, TN: Abingdon Press, 2016.